200 great containers

200 great containers

hamlyn **all color**

Joanna Smith

An Hachette UK company
www.hachette.co.uk

First published in Great Britain in 2009 by Hamlyn,
a division of Octopus Publishing Group Ltd
2–4 Heron Quays, London E14 4JP
www.octopusbooksusa.com

Copyright © Octopus Publishing Group Ltd 2009

Distributed in the U.S. and Canada by Octopus Books USA:
c/o Hachette Book Group
237 Park Avenue
New York NY 10017

ISBN: 978-0-600-62033-4

Printed and bound in China

1 2 3 4 5 6 7 8 9 10

contents

introduction

introduction

Containers are the ultimate in instant gardening. In just a few hours it is possible to create a number of different container displays, and that includes a trip to the nursery or garden center to buy the ingredients. And if you choose the containers and plants well, they look good immediately and can transform your patio area, creating a big visual impact.

Containers are also the ultimate in easy-care gardening. There is no digging involved, no problems with encroaching perennial weeds, and as the plants are not at ground level there is less back-breaking bending. It is also easier to tend plants when they are growing in a container, as you can control the moisture, nutrients, and soil and give them the conditions they like best.

There are two types of container display. First, there are the permanent plantings that stay the same throughout the year—for example, a handsome, evergreen shrub underplanted with perennials to add summer color. Then there are the temporary displays designed for a specific season, using only plants that are at their best at that moment. Permanent plantings involve less work and can look good year-round, but temporary displays allow more scope in terms of creativity, and you can be experimental as you'll only have to live with the results of your decisions for a short while.

This book contains 200 ideas for great permanent and temporary container displays, from flower-filled hanging baskets of summer bedding to year-round containers of shrubs and perennials. They feature a wide range of different plants, from all the summer favorites, such as pelargoniums and petunias, to grasses, vegetables, and some rather more exotic subjects. Use the ideas as recipes to be followed carefully or as inspiration to create your own unique combinations. But most of all just enjoy yourself—you can always change it if you don't like it.

KEY TO SYMBOLS

 site in full sun

 site in partial shade

 site in shade

 plant may be damaged below 23°F (-5°C)

 plant may be damaged by temperatures below 41°F (5°C)

 requires plenty of watering

 requires moderate water

 fertilize regularly

 requires extra care

choosing containers

Containers come in lots of different shapes and sizes, but as long as they hold potting soil they are suitable for accommodating plants. There are a few practical and aesthetic pointers to help you choose.

size

The size of the container will largely be dictated by the position in which it is going to stand: it needs to be in scale with its surroundings. On the whole, fewer, larger containers work better in a space than lots of little ones, as larger containers have more presence. In addition, of course, they are easier to tend, as they contain a larger volume of soil, requiring less frequent fertilizing and watering.

material

The material you choose—terra-cotta, glazed, wooden, galvanized—will partly depend on the style of the surroundings, whether sleek and contemporary or traditional, cottage-style garden. However, there are also practical considerations to take into account. The main one is whether a pot is porous or not: the soil in a terra-cotta pot dries out quickly, making it impracticable for moisture-loving plants like hostas but perfect for alpines, which hate wet soil. You can line porous containers with plastic to help them retain moisture. Wooden

planters will rot unless they are protected, so either use a plastic liner or treat the wood with a water-repellent product. They will still, however, have a limited life.

shape

The main thing to consider when choosing the shape of a container is the volume of potting soil that it will contain: the less soil the more maintenance work involved. Here are a few things to keep in mind:

• Shallow bowls contain less potting soil than deeper pots.

• Troughs and window boxes tend to be quite narrow and shallow, so they don't hold a lot of soil and have to be watered and fertilized more frequently.

• Hanging baskets also hold relatively little potting soil, and unless they are lined with plastic or have a rigid plastic base they also dry out extremely quickly.

potting soils

The type and quality of potting soil can make the difference between success and failure, between healthy, bushy plants covered with flowers and a disappointing show with weak, stunted foliage and few blooms.

types of potting soil

There are two main types of potting soils available: those that contain soil and those that don't.

Soil-based potting soils are designed for permanent plantings, as they are heavy (offering good anchorage) and free draining (allowing good aeration). The nutrients are released slowly, and they have a good structure, which withstands the test of time.

Soilless mixes, which are usually based on peat moss, are designed for temporary plant displays. They are light and easy to use, but the structure breaks down quite quickly, and they soon decrease in volume. They do not hold nutrients well, so you have to fertilize more often, and they are prone to waterlogging in wet weather and dry out quickly in dry weather.

When planting a container with a temporary display, it is a good idea to use a 50:50 mixture of soil-based and soilless mix to reap the benefits of both and make life easier. The soil-based potting mix provides good drainage and stability, while the soilless one makes the mixture more moisture-retentive. Try to find a peat-free soilless mix—an environmentally-friendly product that does not encourage the depletion of peat beds.

Acidic soil mixes are soil-based potting mixes formulated for growing acid-loving plants such as rhododendrons and heaths. These plants will not grow well in all-purpose potting mixes.

extra ingredients

Some plants do best with a little extra care in the form of additional ingredients. Ferns and hostas, for example, thrive in a moist growing mix so will benefit if you add some well-rotted compost or animal manure to their potting mix, to improve water-retention. A third by volume is about right.

Alpines and succulent plants, on the other hand, prefer an extremely free-draining growing medium, so it is a good idea to add about a third by volume of fine gravel or grit to the potting soil to amend the drainage.

all-important drainage

It is vital to get the growing medium correct, but you also need to ensure that moisture can drain adequately out of the container. Check that your container has sufficient drainage holes in the base, and if there aren't enough make some more with a drill.

planting a container

No matter what type of pot, potting soil, and plants you have, the basic method for planting a container is the same. It is worth spending a little time to give your plants the best possible start.

1 Start by watering the plants thoroughly to make sure their rootballs are moist right through. Place pebbles or pieces of broken flowerpot over the drainage holes in the base of the pot, to prevent the soil from being washed out. Start filling the pot with potting mix, firming lightly as you go. Stand the largest plant, still in its pot, on the mix to check the level: the top of the rootball should come about 1½ in. (4 cm) below the rim of the pot. Adjust the soil mix if necessary.

2 Plan your arrangement with the plants still in their pots. Move them around until you are happy with the layout. If it's a temporary display, arrange the plants close together, to give maximum impact straight away. If it's a permanent planting, space the plants so they have room to grow. When you are happy, start removing the plants from their pots by turning each pot upside down while supporting the soil with your fingers, which will be either side of the plant.

3 Add more potting mix to the pot, packing it lightly round each rootball as you go, and firming gently. The plants should end up with the tops of their rootballs level with the top of the soil. Firm the soil lightly between each plant, checking for any gaps. Aim for the top of the soil mix to come 1½ in. (4 cm) below the pot rim, to allow space for watering.

4 Add a layer of mulch if you like. This will suppress weeds, help retain moisture, and add a finishing touch, especially important if there is bare soil visible between the plants. Water the pot thoroughly using a watering can with a waterbreaker. This will prevent the soil from being displaced as you water the plants.

planting a hanging basket

There are two types of hanging basket: those with solid sides, which are planted in the same way as any other container, and those with open sides through which plants can grow. Here's how to plant the latter.

1 First line the basket to prevent the potting mix falling out. You can use moss, cocoa fiber, or synthetic fiber, all of which are built up in layers as you fill the basket; or a one-piece liner, such as burlap, molded paper, or a specially designed hanging basket liner through which you need to make holes for the plants. Place a small saucer in the base of the basket, to help retain moisture.

2 Place a little potting mix in the base of the basket and start positioning the lowest layer of plants, working the foliage through the holes in the sides of the basket from inside out. Add more potting mix as necessary, firming it around the rootball of each plant, then start on the next row of plants higher up the basket sides. Continue up the sides of the basket.

3 When the basket is full, plant the last few plants in the potting mix in the top and firm lightly to make sure there are no air gaps. Try to make the soil in the center of the basket slightly lower than that at the sides, to make watering easier. Water the basket thoroughly using a watering can fitted with a waterbreaker.

4 Insert slow-release fertilizer pellets into the top of the potting mix if you like. These release nutrients slowly and help make sure the plants are well fertilized. Hanging baskets contain a lot of plants for the volume of potting soil, so this is a good idea.

siting containers

There are both practical and aesthetic considerations to be taken into account when siting containers, so think carefully before you place them.

pleasing the plants

Unless you have chosen plants to suit the position of an existing container, you will need to place your container where the plants will thrive. Shade-loving plants will obviously need a shady site and sun-worshippers a sunny one, but also keep in mind whether the spot is sheltered or exposed to cold winds, the worst of the winter wet, or heavy frosts. Buildings can channel winds in unlikely directions, and some plants will not do well in a continual draft.

pleasing the eye

Position is everything when it comes to getting the maximum visual impact out of your containers.

- Small containers, or those with small, intricate plants, should be placed where they can be appreciated at close quarters. Site them on a table on the deck, on top of a low wall, on a plinth, on a doorstep or just somewhere you pass by often.
- Larger pots can play many different roles in the overall design of your garden or patio. Use them as focal points to add drama—

perhaps standing a container at the point where two paths cross or at the end of a vista to create a full stop. They can also be used in pairs to frame a doorway, archway, or even an attractive view.

- Containers are also the perfect solution for softening an otherwise austere feature like a bare house wall or a large expanse of deck. Place a large pot overflowing with foliage and flowers there, and it becomes a garden.
- A handsome plant in a container can also be used to draw the eye away from an ugly feature like trashcan storage, heating system units, or composters. It doesn't need to the hide the feature; just having it nearby will divert attention.
- Containers can also be used to enhance flights of steps. Use a series of identical containers, one to a step on each side, to frame the steps and add drama, or cluster small groups of little pots at the sides of the steps, to add interest and soften the effect.
- A pair of large containers is perfect for framing a feature such as a doorway, gateway, or arch to emphasize it.
- When positioning, think about whether to group your containers or to use them singly. A single, large container has a more dramatic presence and works well as a design feature in its own right. A group of pots has a more informal look.

19

container care

Caring for plants growing in containers is much like caring for plants elsewhere in the garden, but it is important to keep in mind that they rely on you for moisture and nutrients because they cannot draw them from the surrounding soil.

fertilizing

The nutrient requirements of plants vary enormously.

• Shrubs and perennials in pots with a fair amount of soil will be happy with a dose of slow-release fertilizer each year. Fork a little bonemeal or a granular fertilizer into the top of the potting soil in spring.

• Annuals, fast-growing perennials grown for their flowers, and vegetables will need regular fertilizing to encourage strong growth and a succession of blooms or fruits. Liquid fertilizers are convenient to use: simply add the required measure to the water when you are watering. Alternatively, do it automatically by inserting fertilizer pellets into the potting soil when you plant. They release nutrients slowly over a number of weeks.

watering

Even when it rains, container plants receive little moisture so you need to get in the habit of regular watering. Here are a few pointers to make it easier:

• Consider installing an automatic watering system with a timer if you have lots of containers but little spare time.

• Add moisture-retaining crystals to the potting soil when you plant if there is going to be lots of plants in a small space.

• Make sure the level of the potting soil is at least 1 in. (2.5 cm) below the rim of the container so you can really soak the soil when you water.

• Stand pots in saucers. It really helps to conserve moisture.

deadheading

Removing the dead blooms of annuals and most perennials as they fade is vital if you want to encourage them to produce more. As soon as an annual sets seed, its job is done, so it stops flowering and dies. Keep deadheading and give them a reason to produce more flowers.

repotting

Plants growing in containers for more than a year or two will need to be repotted when they outgrow their space. Simply remove them from the current pot, gently break up the outer edges of the rootball to remove some of the old soil, and repot into fresh potting soil, using a slightly larger container if appropriate.

spring collection

spring beauties

You need

20 *Tulipa* 'Angélique' bulbs **A**

5 *Myosotis sylvatica*
(forget-me-not) **B**

A dazzling array of lovely, pastel pink tulips and soft blue forget-me-nots in a half-barrel is the very essence of spring.

Planting & care Plant the half-barrel in the fall. Fill it to 8 in. (20 cm) below the rim with a free-draining potting mix. Arrange the tulip bulbs on top of the mix with the pointed ends uppermost. Add another 6 in. (15 cm) of soil mix on top and firm lightly. Plant the forget-me-nots, evenly spaced, in the top of the pot. Keep the potting mix just moist. After flowering, fertilize the bulbs with a liquid fertilizer, to plump them up for next year. Remove the forget-me-nots and replace them with summer bedding.

Or you could try a cool and elegant, all-white display with white forget-me-nots and white tulips, such as the simple 'Purissima', the green-based 'Spring Green', or the frilly 'White Parrot'.

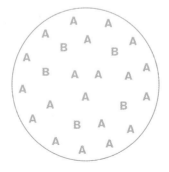

beautiful ballerinas

You need

5 *Tulipa* 'Queen of Night' bulbs **A**

15 *Tulipa* 'Ballerina' bulbs **B**

2 *Skimmia japonica* cultivars **C**

3 *Hedera helix* cultivars (variegated ivy) **D**

3 *Pennisetum alopecuroides* 'Hameln' (fountain grass) **E**

Vibrant orange tulip 'Ballerina' is shown to good advantage against a backdrop of pinky skimmia and the brown winter foliage of spiky fountain grass. This container is designed to be viewed from one side only, perfect for positioning in front of a hedge, fence, or wall.

Planting & care Plant the pot in the fall, using a free-draining potting mix. Fill the pot to 8 in. (20 cm) below the rim and arrange the bulbs on top of the potting mix, pointed ends up. Add another 6 in. (15 cm) of mix, firm lightly, and plant the other plants in the top. Keep just moist over winter, then water regularly in spring and summer. Fertilize the pot plants in early summer after the bulbs have flowered.

Or you could try cream-colored daffodils, such as 'Canisp' or 'Cool Crystal', instead of the tulips for a more muted display.

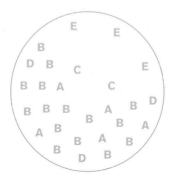

primrose basket

You need

3 *Primula* Wanda Supreme
Series (primroses) **A**

8 *Crocus* 'Vanguard'
(Dutch crocus) bulbs **B**

This pretty, woven wall basket is overflowing with dainty, lilac crocuses and pink primroses, perfect for cheering up a plain wall in early spring. Plant up a number of baskets and hang them close together for a fuller display.

Planting & care Plant the basket in the fall. Line it with polyethylene sheeting and make a drainage hole in the base. Fill with free-draining potting mix and plant the primroses in the top. Use a dibble or stick to make holes between the primroses for the bulbs: they should be planted about 2 in. (5 cm) below the surface, pointed ends up. Cover with more potting mix and keep moist over winter. After the flowers have finished, plant out the crocuses and primroses in the garden and fill the basket with summer bedding.

Or you could try a summer display of ivy-leaved pelargoniums in the basket, which would thrive in the dry conditions a small amount of potting mix provides. 'L'Elégante' has white flowers and lovely, silvery foliage with cream and pink variegations.

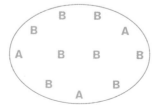

basket of bulbs

You need

10 *Tulipa* 'Stresa' bulbs **A**

30 *Crocus ancyrensis* bulbs **B**

A simple rattan hanging basket is filled with golden crocuses and smart, yellow and red tulip 'Stresa', bringing a ray of sunshine and a cheerful note to the yard in early spring.

Planting & care Plant the hanging basket in the fall. Line it with a piece of polyethylene and make some holes in it. Fill to within 6 in. (15 cm) of the rim with a free-draining potting mix, then arrange the tulip bulbs, pointed ends up, on top. Add another 3 in. (8 cm) of mix and arrange the crocus bulbs around the edges of the basket. Fill the basket with potting mix to within 1 in. (2.5 cm) of the rim, and firm lightly. Keep just moist over winter. After the bulbs have finished flowering, plant them in the garden and fill the basket with bedding plants.

Or you could try a pink and purple planting design with deep pink tulip 'Pink Diamond' and purple-pink crocus 'Ruby Giant'.

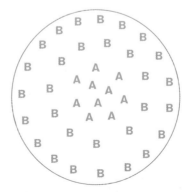

the scent of spring

You need

10 *Narcissus* 'Bridal Crown'
  (daffodil) bulbs **A**

6 *Viola* cultivars (pansy) **B**

4 *Hedera helix* cultivars (ivy) **C**

A simple, terra-cotta pot is ideal to enhance a gorgeous group of 'Bridal Crown' daffodils, with their intoxicating scent. Cream pansies and cream-splashed ivy soften the effect.

Planting & care Plant the pot in the fall, using a free-draining potting mix. Fill the pot to within 8 in. (20 cm) of the rim and arrange the daffodils on top, pointed ends up. Add 6 in. (15 cm) of potting mix and firm lightly, then plant the pansies and ivy in the top. Keep moist over winter, and apply a liquid fertilizer when the daffodils finish flowering. Remove the pansies when they finish flowering and replace with summer bedding. Plant new pansies in the pot the following fall.

Or you could try replacing the pansies with pretty, white *Anemone blanda* (windflower). Plant the bulbs about 2 in. (5 cm) below the surface of the potting mix.

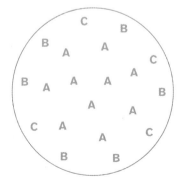

double the pleasure

You need

10 *Tulipa* 'Blue Diamond' bulbs **A**

1 *Euphorbia amygdaloides* 'Purpurea' (spurge) **B**

1 *Phlomis italica* **C**

1 *Viola* 'Magnifico' **D**

1 *Hedera helix* cultivar (ivy) **E**

1 *Polemonium caeruleum* 'Brise d'Anjou' (variegated Jacob's ladder) **F**

1 *Corydalis flexuosa* 'Purple Leaf' **G**

This lovely container of perennials, annuals, and bulbs for late spring includes gorgeous, double tulips, bright green euphorbia, silvery, felted phlomis, and blue corydalis, an intricate mix of colors, textures, and forms.

Planting & care Plant the pot in the fall, using a free-draining potting mix. Fill the pot to 8 in. (20 cm) below the rim, then arrange the tulip bulbs on top of the mix, pointed ends up. Add more potting mix, to just below the pot rim, and plant the other plants in the top. Keep just moist over winter. Apply a liquid fertilizer when the tulip flowers fade. The phlomis and polemonium will go on to flower in the summer, so keep watering regularly and enjoy a second show.

Or you could try replacing the tulips with ornamental onion bulbs, which flower a little later. *Allium caeruleum* has bright blue, rounded flowerheads, while *A. rosenbachianum* has gorgeous, deep purple flowers.

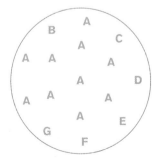

spring cheer

You need

15 *Tulipa* 'Peach Blossom'
bulbs **A**

15 *Narcissus* (daffodil)
bulbs **B**

15 *Primula vulgaris* cultivars
(primroses) **C**

4 *Scilla siberica* (spring
squill) bulbs **D**

This bright and cheerful, window-box display of primroses and spring bulbs in a range of vivid colors will certainly blow away the cobwebs.

Planting & care Plant the window box in the fall, using a free-draining potting mix. Fill the box to 6 in. (15 cm) below the rim, and arrange the tulip and daffodil bulbs on top. Add another 5 in. (12 cm) of potting mix, firm lightly, and plant the primroses in the top. Make holes 2 in. (5 cm) deep with your finger, and pop in the scilla bulbs, pointed ends up. Refill the holes. Keep the mix just moist over winter. After the plants have finished flowering, transplant the bulbs and primroses to the garden.

Or you could try an all-yellow window-box display, using yellow tulips, such as the double-flowered 'Monte Carlo' or the elegant, single 'Sweet Harmony', with sunny yellow daffodils and all-yellow primroses.

B	A	B	B	C	B	A	B	B	A	B	A	B
C	C	A	A	B	C	C	A	B	A	B	C	A
A	B	C	C	C	B	A	C	C	A	C		
C	C	A	D	A	B	D	D	C	D	B	A	

cheeky faces

You need

10 *Viola* (mixed, smaller-
flowered viola) **A**

A visit to the garden center in spring will reveal a whole range of cute, little violas, with faces of all colors. Pick a selection of your favorites and plant them in a simple, terra-cotta bowl, which won't detract from their pretty colors and intricate markings.

Planting & care Plant the violas in spring in a free-draining potting mix, and place the bowl in sun or partial shade. Water and fertilize regularly to keep the violas going: they should provide a colorful display right through the spring and summer. Remove and discard the plants when they become long and straggly and produce fewer flowers, or shear off the foliage, fertilize and water well, and wait for them to shoot again.

Or you could try filling the bowl with heartsease (*Viola tricolor*), the wild pansy, for a simpler, cottage-garden-style look. The flowers have pretty, little, yellow, deep purple, and white faces.

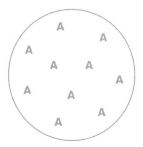

cool cream and white

You need

1 *Helleborus niger* (Christmas rose) **A**

5 *Hyacinthus orientalis* 'City of Haarlem' (hyacinth) bulbs **B**

1 *Acorus gramineus* 'Ogon' (Japanese rush) **C**

1 *Silene uniflora* 'Druett's Variegated' (variegated bladder campion) **D**

2 *Erica carnea* 'Springwood White' (winter heath) **E**

This sophisticated, early spring display uses white heaths and a hellebore with creamy hyacinths. The flowers are enhanced by the variegated foliage of Japanese rush and bladder campion, a great combination of shapes and patterns in a muted color range.

Planting & care Plant the pot in the fall, using a free-draining, moisture-retentive potting mix. The hyacinth bulbs should be planted about 4 in. (10 cm) below the surface of the potting mix. Keep just moist over winter. Fertilize with a liquid fertilizer in midspring, as the hyacinth flowers fade. All these plants are perennial and can be kept in the container from year to year. The bladder campion produces lovely, white flowers in summer.

Or you could try a display of blue, white, and gray, using *Silene uniflora* 'Robin Whitebreast' with gray-green foliage, *Festuca glauca* (blue fescue) instead of the Japanese rush, and deep blue hyacinths, such as 'Delft Blue' or 'Blue Jacket'.

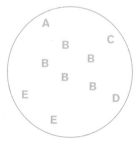

pink perfection

A lovely, weathered, terra-cotta trough contains gorgeous, blousy, peony-flowered tulips and wonderful, deep pink ranunculus—a simple but effective display for late spring.

You need

10 double late tulip bulbs, such as 'Angélique' or 'Maywonder' **A**

8 pink ranunculus **B**

Planting & care Plant the trough in the fall, using free-draining, moisture-retentive potting mix. Fill the trough to 6 in. (15 cm) below the rim with mix and arrange the tulip bulbs on top, pointed ends up. Add another 4 in. (10 cm) of potting mix, and firm lightly. Plant the ranunculus plants in the top, arranged along the front of the trough. Keep the potting mix just moist over winter. Fertilize with a liquid fertilizer when the tulips have finished flowering. Discard the ranunculus when they stop flowering, and plant the tulips in the garden.

Or you could try a more vibrant display of bright orange or yellow ranunculus with tulip 'Golden Artist', a rich orange tulip with green stripes up the backs of the petals, or tulip 'Allegretto', a big, bright double tulip with red and orange flowers.

	A		A		A		A		A
A		A		A		A		A	
		B			B		B		B
B			B			B		B	

citrus shades

You need

1 *Euphorbia characias* subsp. *wulfenii* (spurge) **A**

6 *Viola* (orange, smaller-flowered viola) **B**

Lime-green euphorbia and bright orange violas make a pleasing contrast in a plain and simple, terra-cotta pot, a zesty combination of colors for late spring.

Planting & care Plant the pot in the fall or early spring, using a free-draining potting mix. Choose a bushy euphorbia plant with a number of stems for a full display, or plant three smaller plants in the pot. Plant the violas around the euphorbia, and topdress the pot with a layer of grit or fine gravel, to set off the plants and suppress weeds. Keep the potting mix just moist, and remove the dead flowerheads from the violas, to encourage them to produce more flowers.

Or you could try *Euphorbia griffithii* 'Fireglow' with its bright orange flowers and red-tinged foliage. Choose orange violas for a harmonious display or clear blue violas for a striking contrast.

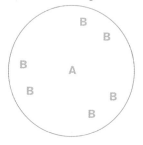

stripy irises

You need

1 *Iris pseudacorus* 'Variegata'
(yellow flag) **A**

This towering and stately iris makes an elegant subject for a simple, green, glazed pot. The handsome, striped foliage looks good from spring to the fall, while the pretty, yellow flowers are a bonus in late spring.

Planting & care Plant the pot at any time of year using a rich, moisture-retentive potting soil, mixed with some well-rotted compost or manure if you can. This iris needs moist, even wet, soil so use a glazed pot to retain moisture and stand it in a saucer of water. As it grows quickly, one plant is enough to fill the pot. Fork in some bonemeal or other slow-release fertilizer each year in early spring.

Or you could try growing another moisture-loving iris, such as *Iris laevigata* with purple flowers, *I. l.* var. *alba* with white flowers or *I. l.* 'Rosea' with pink flowers.

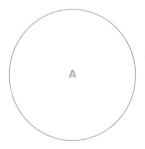

true blue

You need

15 *Muscari armeniacum* (grape hyacinth) bulbs **A**

3 *Milium effusum* 'Aureum' (golden wood millet) **B**

True blue grape hyacinths are set off to good advantage by the newly emerging, lime-green leaves of golden wood millet. As the bulbs die down, the grass will fill the basket with soft, bright foliage until the fall.

Planting & care Plant the basket in the fall, using a moisture-retentive potting mix. Plant the golden wood millets first, equally spaced in the basket, then poke the muscari bulbs into the mix around them, with the convex, more pointed ends up. The bulbs should be about 2 in. (5 cm) below the surface of the potting mix. Keep just moist over winter. Fertilize with a liquid fertilizer after the bulbs have flowered.

Or you could try growing white grape hyacinths (*Muscari botryoides* 'Album') underplanted with the black grassy foliage of *Ophiopogon planiscapus* 'Nigrescens'.

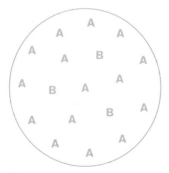

classical elegance

You need

3 *Helleborus orientalis* (lenten rose) **A**

3 *Hyacinthus orientalis* (hyacinth) bulbs **B**

3 *Primula vulgaris* cultivars (primroses) **C**

3 *Hedera helix* cultivars (ivy) **D**

Graceful, pink lenten roses rise above cute, faded pink primroses and light pink hyacinths in a classical, terra-cotta pot. The rim of the pot has been softened by trails of red-tinged ivy, wrapped loosely around the edges.

Planting & care Plant the pot in the fall, using a moisture-retentive potting mix. Plant the hellebores first, then sink the hyacinth bulbs into the potting mix between them, pointed ends up, about 4 in. (10 cm) deep. Plant the primroses and ivies around the edges of the pot, then wrap the ivy trails loosely around the pot rim. Keep moist over winter, then apply a liquid fertilizer as the plants come into flower. Fertilize again in early summer and keep the potting mix just moist.

Or you could try creating the same display in shades of soft yellow, with *Helleborus* x *hybridus* 'Citron', pale yellow primroses and hyacinths, and *Hedera helix* 'Buttercup' with its lovely, golden foliage.

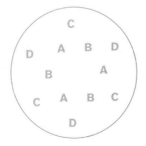

spring sunshine

You need

1 *Ilex aquifolium* (holly) **A**

3 *Lonicera nitida* 'Baggesen's Gold' (honeysuckle) **B**

3 *Viola* cultivars (pansy) **C**

8 *Tulipa* 'West Point' bulbs **D**

This sunny, spring display includes yellow, lily-flowered tulips, yellow pansies, and golden-leaved honeysuckle, with holly to add height and structure. Replace the pansies with fresh plants when they finish flowering, and you can keep the display going year-round.

Planting & care Plant the pot in the fall, using a free-draining potting mix. Arrange the holly in the middle and the three honeysuckles evenly spaced around the sides. Plant the tulip bulbs in a ring around the holly, pointed ends up and about 4 in. (10 cm) deep. Lastly, pop the pansies between the honeysuckle plants and firm the potting mix well. Keep the soil just moist, and fertilize with a liquid fertilizer as the tulip flowers fade.

Or you could try a blue and white display with *Ilex aquifolium* 'Argentea Marginata' (a pretty holly with white-edged leaves), green-leaved *Lonicera nitida*, bright white pansies, and tulip 'Blue Parrot'.

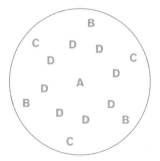

cheerful contrast

You need

6 *Viola* cultivars (pansy) **A**

6 *Anemone blanda* 'Blue Star' (windflower) bulbs **B**

Cheerful, orange pansies and bright blue windflowers make a pleasing contrast for early spring. The plain, terra-cotta pot has a distressed turquoise paint finish, to enhance the vivid colors of the display.

Planting & care Plant the pot in the fall, using a free-draining potting mix. Fill the pot to 4 in. (10 cm) below the rim and arrange the anemone bulbs in a group in the middle, on top of the soil. Add another 2 in. (5 cm) of potting mix and plant the pansies equally spaced around the edges of the pot. Keep just moist over winter, and apply a liquid fertilize as the plants come into flower. Discard the pansies when they finish flowering, and plant the anemone bulbs in the garden.

Or you could try different contrasting colors, such as white *Anemone blanda* 'White Splendor' with deep purple/black pansies; or bright pink *A. b.* 'Pink Star' with golden-yellow pansies, a dazzling combination.

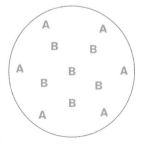

simplicity itself

You need

20 *Viola* cultivars (pansy) **A**

While it's tempting to combine a whole range of different plants in a container, this display proves that understatement can work just as well. There's enough variation in the color of the pansies to add interest, but they are similar enough to create a harmonious whole.

Planting & care Plant the pot in spring just as the young pansy plants are coming into flower so you can see exactly what colors you have. Choose a range of plants with flowers of a similar color but with some variation in the shade. Use a free-draining potting mix, and space the plants equally in the container. Keep the potting mix just moist, and fertilize from time to time with a liquid fertilizer, to keep the plants blooming. Removing the spent flowerheads will extend the flowering period. Discard the plants when they have finished flowering.

Or you could try an *en masse* planting of spring-flowering English daisies (*Bellis perennis*) with their charming, pompon flowers. Choose all-pink- or all-white-flowered plants—the doubles are especially attractive.

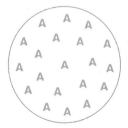

summer stunners

contrasting colors

You need

1 *Helictotrichon sempervirens* (blue oat grass) **A**

2 *Helianthemum* cultivar (rock rose) **B**

2 *Tagetes* cultivar (French marigold) **C**

A pleasing contrast of blue oat grass and orange rock roses and marigolds fills a pretty, glazed bowl. This display is best placed in a raised position, so the color and pleasing shape of the bowl can be best appreciated.

Planting & care Plant the container in late spring after all risk of frost has passed, using a free-draining potting mix. Keep the potting mix on the dry side, and apply a liquid fertilizer from time to time throughout the summer, to keep the marigolds flowering. Remove the dead marigold flowers as they fade, to encourage more to come. Discard the marigolds when they finish flowering. The grass and rock roses are perennials, so transfer them to the garden in the fall, or leave them in the bowl and add fresh marigolds next spring.

Or you could try a red and blue display using deep red rock roses and red or mahogany marigolds, such as 'Mars' or 'Red Cherry'.

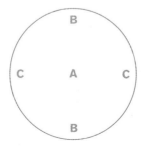

scarlet fire

You need

3 *Pelargonium* Belle Cascade 'Red' (geranium) **A**

2 *Antirrhinum* Bells 'Red' (snapdragon) **B**

3 *Fuchsia* 'Marinka' **C**

8 *Petunia* 'Surfinia Red' **D**

8 *Diascia barberae* 'Ruby Field' **E**

4 *Lobelia* 'Rosamund' **F**

4 *Verbena* Sandy Series 'Red' **G**

4 *Glechoma hederacea* 'Variegata' **H**

This dramatic hanging basket, with its bold array of brilliant red flowers, would make a stunning focal point in any summer garden. For maximum effect, try hanging it on a white wall or against a backdrop of a dark green hedge or fence.

Planting & care Plant the basket in late spring, after all risk of frost has passed, using a moisture-retentive potting mix to which you have added some moisture-retaining crystals. Insert some slow-release fertilizer pellets into the potting mix, because there are a lot of plants in this basket and they will need plenty of nutrients to grow and flower well. Water regularly, and remove dead flowerheads as they fade, to encourage more blooms.

Or you could try using the same plants in a window box, where they would cascade gracefully over the sill and down the wall below.

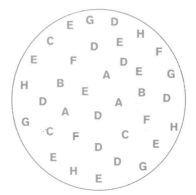

bountiful basket

You need

2 *Petunia* 'Duo' **A**

2 *Nemesia* 'Burning Embers' **B**

1 *Pelargonium* cultivar (geranium) **C**

3 *Viola* cultivar (pansy) **D**

8 *Lobelia erinus* 'Cascade Mixed' **E**

3 *Glechoma hederacea* 'Variegata' **F**

2 *Helichrysum petiolare* 'Variegatum' **G**

This pretty basket contains an unashamed mixture of summer flowers in all shapes and colors. It shows just what can be achieved by disregarding design principles and simply picking what pleases you.

Planting & care Plant the basket in late spring, when all risk of frost has passed, using a moisture-retentive potting mix. Insert fertilizer pellets into the potting mix, to nourish the plants. Water regularly, because baskets dry out quickly. Remove dead flowers as they fade, to encourage more blooms throughout the summer.

Or you could try limiting the display to just lobelia 'Cascade Mixed', relying on the different shades of pink, purple, blue, and white to add interest. You would need 15–20 plants for a basket of this size.

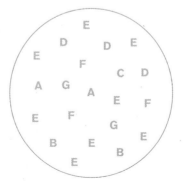

summer sun

You need

1 *Argyranthemum* 'Schone von Nizza' **A**

1 *Tagetes* cultivar (French marigold) **B**

1 *Nemesia* 'Nemesis Orange' **C**

2 *Helichrysum petiolare* 'Silver Mini' **D**

A sunshine-yellow window box has been planted with a group of sunny plants—argyranthemum with its yellow, daisy flowers, French marigold, and orange-yellow nemesia. The blue-green foliage makes a pleasing contrast to the yellows.

Planting & care Plant the window box in late spring, when all risk of frost has passed, using a free-draining, moisture-retentive potting mix. Place in a sunny site, and keep the potting mix just moist. Apply a liquid fertilizer every two weeks, while the plants are in flower. Remove the flowers of the marigold and argyranthemum as they fade, to encourage the plants to produce more blooms.

Or you could try limiting the color range even more with a pure yellow nemesia. Team up with lime-green *Helichrysum petiolare* 'Limelight'.

dazzling daisies

You need

1 *Argyranthemum* 'Jamaica Primrose' **A**

2 *Verbena* Sandy Series 'Red' **B**

2 *Calibrachoa* Million Bells 'Yellow' **C**

1 *Abutilon* Bella Series **D**

2 *Osteospermum* cultivar **E**

The plain, square lines of this terra-cotta pot are the perfect foil for a full display of tender perennials in shades of red, orange, and yellow. With regular deadheading, these plants will flower right through summer and into the fall.

Planting & care Plant the pot in late spring, when all risk of frost has passed, using a free-draining potting mix. Keep the mix just moist, and apply a liquid fertilizer every two weeks. Deadhead the plants regularly, to encourage them to produce more flowers. All these plants are tender perennials, so you can either let them die off in the winter and start with fresh plants next spring, or you can move the pot to a frost-free greenhouse to keep them alive. Cut back hard in spring, and fertilize and water well for a repeat performance next summer.

Or you could try combining the same plants in shades of pink, including pale pink *Argyranthemum* 'Vancouver', deep pink *Verbena* 'Sissinghurst', *Calibrachoa* Million Bells 'Pink', *Abutilon* 'Louis Marignac', and *Osteospermum* 'Daisy Mae'.

scarlet spikes

You need

3 *Mimulus* (monkey flower) **A**

2 *Imperata cylindrica* 'Rubra' (Japanese blood grass) **B**

A colorful combination of scarlet Japanese blood grass and bright yellow monkey flower makes a great show in summer. Team up with pots of different grasses for a varied and architectural collection in a sunny spot.

Planting & care Plant the pot in late spring, when all risk of frost has passed, using a moisture-retentive potting mix. Stand in a sunny place, and water regularly—both plants like moist soil. Remove the flowers from the mimulus as they fade, to encourage more blooms to come.

Or you could try replacing the yellow mimulus with a bright red one, to match the blood grass. Alternatively, try some of the other handsome grasses, such as zebra grass (*Miscanthus sinensis* 'Zebrinus') with its tall, green foliage banded with yellow, the bronze-leaved *Carex flagellifera*, or the stripy *Carex oshimensis* 'Evergold', which makes a pretty mound of soft foliage.

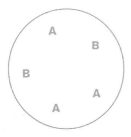

pretty pastels

You need

2 *Salvia farinacea* cultivar
  (mealycup sage) **A**

3 *Campanula carpatica*
  (bellflower) **B**

2 *Lobelia erinus* cultivar **C**

1 *Verbena* Sandy Series
  'Pink' **D**

A simple, white window box has been planted with an endearing array of pretty, pastel pink and blue, tender perennials, which will flower all summer long. Be sure to choose a compact verbena cultivar and an edging lobelia to form neat, floriferous mounds.

Planting & care Plant the window box in late spring, when all risk of frost has passed. Use a moisture-retentive potting mix, and insert some fertilizer pellets to make sure the nutrient levels are kept up, to encourage plenty of flowers. Deadhead regularly.

Or you could try an all-blue window box using fairy fan-flower (*Scaevola aemula*) instead of the pink verbena. This trailing plant has pretty heads of blue, fan-shaped flowers right through summer and into the fall.

vivid shades

You need

3 *Erysimum* cultivar
 (wallflower) **A**

2 *Euphorbia amygdaloides*
 var. *robbiae* (spurge) **B**

2 *Carex oshimensis* 'Evergold'
 (sedge) **C**

This eye-catching, early-summer pot contains a vivid array of bright colors: lime-green spurge, stripy-yellow sedge, and the brilliant flowers of erysimum in vibrant pink, rich orange, and yellow all on the same plant.

Planting & care Plant the pot when the wallflowers are available, using a free-draining, moisture-retentive potting mix. Use either one or three wallflowers in the middle of the pot, depending on its size. Trim back the wallflowers after flowering, and remove the spurge heads as they start to look untidy. Fork a little bonemeal or other slow-release fertilizer into the top of the potting mix each spring.

Or you could try a purple wallflower such as *Erysimum* 'Bowles's Mauve' with the lime-green spurge, and use a lime-green grass such as golden wood millet (*Milium effusum* 'Aureum') instead of the stripy sedge.

pretty in purple

You need

6 *Verbena* cultivar **A**

3 *Xerochrysum bracteatum* cultivar (strawflower) **B**

3 *Helichrysum petiolare* 'Limelight' **C**

A sea of pretty, purple verbena is made more vivid by the contrast of the orange and yellow strawflowers nestling among it and the fiery lotus hanging down from the pot above. Lime-green helichrysum lightens the design.

Planting & care Plant the pot in late spring, when all risk of frost has passed, using a free-draining potting mix. Keep the potting mix moist, and apply a liquid fertilizer every two weeks or so. Deadhead the strawflowers and verbenas regularly, to keep the flowers coming.

Or you could try combining gray-leaved *Helichrysum petiolare* with the purple verbena and replacing the strawflowers with a fluffy, blue *Ageratum houstonianum* cultivar. Choose a compact variety such as 'Blue Mist' with rich blue flowers.

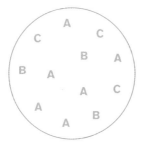

bright begonias

You need

8 *Begonia semperflorens*
cultivar **A**

2 *Lobelia erinus* cultivar **B**

Bedding begonias are perfect for container displays, as they flower all summer long without the need for cosseting. Come rain or shine, they produce their bright flowers in shades of red, pink, and white from late spring to the fall.

Planting & care Plant the trough in late spring, when all risk of frost has passed, using a free-draining, moisture-retentive potting mix. Place the trough in sun or partial shade, and keep the potting mix moist. Apply a liquid fertilizer every two weeks.

Or you could try an elegant, all-white trough, using white lobelias and white begonias.

cascade of color

You need

6 *Mimulus aurantiacus* **A**

4 dwarf *Tropaeolum* cultivar
(nasturtium) **B**

3 *Diascia* cultivar **C**

1 *Phygelius* cultivar **D**

1 *Fuchsia* cultivar **E**

3 *Begonia* tubers **F**

1 *Bidens ferulifolia* **G**

1 *Gazania* cultivar **H**

3 *Verbena* cultivar **I**

2 *Pelargonium* cultivar
(geranium) **J**

1 *Lysimachia nummularia*
'Aurea' (creeping Jenny) **K**

A metal trough has been lined with moss
and planted with a cheerful jumble of trailing
summer flowers in warm shades of red, orange,
and yellow—a positive profusion of bright flowers
and foliage.

Planting & care Start off the begonia tubers in small
pots indoors in late winter. Plant them one to a pot of
water-retentive potting mix, stand on a sunny windowsill,
and keep moist. Plant the trough in late spring when
all risk of frost has passed. Line it with moss and fill
with water-retentive potting mix, to which you have added
some moisture-retaining crystals. Arrange the plants in
the top and sides of the trough, in the same way as you
would when planting a hanging basket. Water the trough
every day, as the potting mix will dry out quickly.

Or you could try growing the same plants in a hanging
basket. All of them have a trailing habit and lend
themselves to baskets.

bronze fountain

You need

1 *Cordyline australis*
(cabbage palm) **A**

4 *Campanula*
portenschlagiana
(Dalmatian bellflower) **B**

A beautiful, bronze-leaved palm rises above a sea of blue campanula in a handsome, square, glazed pot. Although at its best in summer while the campanula is in flower, this container looks good year-round, as both of the plants have evergreen foliage.

Planting & care Plant the container at any time of year, using a moisture-retentive potting mix. Place in sun or partial shade, and sprinkle a little bonemeal or other slow-release fertilizer into the top of the container each year. Trim off any dead leaves from the palm from time to time, and cut back the campanula if it gets untidy.

Or you could try a variegated palm with cream-striped leaves, such as *Cordyline australis* 'Variegata' or 'Torbay Dazzler', with white bellflowers such as *Campanula carpatica* f. *alba* 'Bressingham White'.

summer beauty

You need

1 *Helichrysum petiolare*
  'Rondello' **A**

3 *Scaevola aemula*
  (fairy fan-flower) **B**

2 *Calibrachoa* Celebration
  'Fire' **C**

A plain and elegant pot has been planted with trailing, tender perennials, forming large mounds of foliage and flowers: the burning pinks and oranges of calibrachoa, lovely, purple fairy fan-flower, and the felted, gray foliage of helichrysum.

Planting & care Plant the pot in late spring, when all risk of frost has passed, using a free-draining potting mix. Pinch back the growing tips of the plants when they are young, to encourage them to branch and form dense mounds. Apply a liquid fertilizer every two weeks, and water regularly.

Or you could try combining pink fan-flower (*Scaevola* 'Pink Dream') with purple calibrachoa and plain, gray *Helichrysum petiolare*.

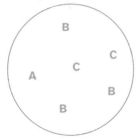

pinks and purples

You need

3 *Pelargonium* 'Frank
Headley' **A**

2 *Helichrysum petiolare* **B**

3 *Fuchsia* cultivar **C**

5 *Diascia* cultivar (2 pale pink,
3 red-pink) **D**

10 *Lobelia erinus* cultivar **E**

4 *Glechoma hederacea*
'Variegata' **F**

A white, wooden window box is overflowing with pretty, pastel pinks and purples, including fancy-leaved geraniums with their smart, cream-and-green foliage. A busy, intricate display like this is best viewed against a plain, white background.

Planting & care Plant the window box in late spring, when all risk of frost has passed, using a free-draining potting mix. Be sure to choose trailing lobelia cultivars, for a full look. Keep moist, and fertilize regularly with a liquid fertilizer, to keep up the display until the fall. Deadhead the geraniums to encourage more blooms to come.

Or you could try some of the other handsome, fancy-leaved geraniums, such as *Pelargonium* 'Mont Blanc', with its brilliant white, silver, and green leaves and white flowers, or 'Pink Dolly Varden', with its pink flowers and leaves marked with pink, green, and cream.

E	A	B	E	A	E	B	A	E
E	D	E	E	D	E	E	D	E
F	C	D	F	C	F	D	C	F

smoldering success

You need

2 *Zinnia elegans* 'Thumbelina' **A**

1 *Tagetes* cultivar (French marigold) **B**

2 *Verbena* Sandy Series 'Scarlet' **C**

2 *Salvia splendens* (scarlet sage) **D**

2 *Calibrachoa* Celebration 'Fire' **E**

Instead of following the usual color rules, this yellow window box has been planted with pinks, oranges, and reds, a clashing blend of rich smoldering colors that combine beautifully.

Planting & care Plant the window box in late spring, when all risk of frost has passed, using a free-draining, moisture-retentive potting mix. Keep moist, and apply a liquid fertilizer every two weeks. Remove the blooms as they fade, to encourage more to appear.

Or you could try replacing the calibrachoa and verbena with *Lantana camara*, a lovely spreading plant rather like a verbena. The flowerheads are a heady mix of shocking pink and orange—perfect to combine with other hot colors.

fresh greens

You need

1 *Cotinus coggygria* 'Golden Spirit' (smoke bush) **A**

1 *Helenium* 'The Bishop' **B**

1 *Lysimachia nummularia* 'Aurea' (creeping Jenny) **C**

1 *Lamium maculatum* 'Golden Anniversary' (deadnettle) **D**

1 *Saxifraga* x *urbium* (London pride) **E**

1 *Hakonechloa macra* 'Alboaurea' **F**

A lovely mixture of perennials and a shrub adorns a vivid blue, glazed pot. The fresh greens and yellows contrast perfectly with the container, creating a bright and striking display for a shady corner in summer.

Planting & care Plant the pot at any time of year, using a moisture-retentive potting mix. Fork a little bonemeal or other slow-release fertilizer into the top of the potting mix each spring. To maintain a show of vivid, lime-green foliage, cut back all of the smoke bush stems to one or two buds from the base in early spring each year. Heleniums flower for a long period in summer and can be encouraged further by deadheading. Trim any dead foliage off the deadnettle, London pride, and grass in early spring, to keep them neat.

Or you could try a similar design in purples and reds, including a purple-leaved smoke bush (*Cotinus coggygria* 'Royal Purple'), dark red *Helenium* 'Moerheim Beauty', creeping, purple-leaved bugleweed (*Ajuga reptans* 'Catlin's Giant'), and red-tinged Japanese blood grass (*Imperata cylindrica* 'Rubra').

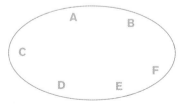

purple passion

You need

2 *Astelia nervosa*
  'Westland' **A**

2 *Osteospermum*
  'Nasinga Purple' **B**

A gorgeous, mosaic-covered trough has inspired this planting of bronze astelias and deep purple osteospermums, a striking combination for a sunny spot.

Planting & care Plant the trough in late spring, when all risk of frost has passed, using a free-draining, moisture-retentive potting mix. Apply a liquid fertilizer every two weeks, and remove the heads of the osteospermums as they fade, to encourage more flowers to come.

Or you could try using green-and-white-striped spider plants (*Chlorophytum comosum* 'Variegatum') instead of the bronze astelias, and *Osteospermum* 'Whirlygig', which has eye-catching, white, crimped flowers with blue backs to the petals.

seed-raised show

You need

1 *Helianthus annuus* cultivar
(dwarf sunflower) **A**

3 *Phlox* 'Bobby Sox' **B**

3 *Tagetes* 'Lemon Gem' **C**

This cheerful potful of annuals has been raised from seed on a windowsill indoors, a cheap and satisfying way to fill the garden and offering a much wider choice of interesting and exciting plants to try.

Planting & care Sow the seeds in early spring, in small pots of seed starter mix. Sprinkle the marigold and phlox seeds on the surface of the starter mix, then sift a little extra mix over the top, to cover lightly. The larger sunflower seeds can be poked individually into the starter mix about 1 in. (2.5 cm) deep. Place upturned, clear polyethylene bags over the pots, and hold in place with rubber bands. Stand on a sunny windowsill, and keep the soil mix just moist. When the seedlings are big enough to handle, transplant into individual pots. Plant the pot in late spring or early summer, when all risk of frost has passed, using a free-draining potting mix, and deadhead regularly, to keep the flowers coming.

Or you could try buying the young plants rather than raising your own from seed.

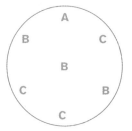

bright white

A dark glazed pot hosts a dazzling display of bright white flowers and foliage, an elegant summer show for sun or partial shade.

You need

1 *Argyranthemum* cultivar **A**

3 *Impatiens walleriana* Accent 'White' (busy Lizzie) **B**

2 *Lobelia erinus* cultivar **C**

1 *Hypoestes* cultivar (polka-dot plant) **D**

Planting & care Plant the pot in late spring, when all risk of frost has passed, using a free-draining, moisture-retentive potting mix. Keep the potting mix just moist, and fertilize every two weeks with a liquid fertilizer. Deadhead the busy Lizzies and argyranthemum regularly, to encourage them to produce more blooms.

Or you could try using the same plants in shades of pastel pink. Try *Argyranthemum* 'Mary Wootton', busy Lizzie Accent 'Pink', pale pink lobelia, and a pretty, pink-spotted polka-dot plant.

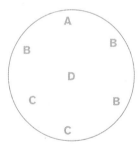

firework display

You need

2 *Pelargonium* 'Fireworks' **A**

1 *Heuchera* cultivar (coral flower) **B**

1 *Nemesia* cultivar **C**

A plain, gray, galvanized pot is the perfect foil for a metallic heuchera, lilac nemesia, and pale pink pelargonium 'Fireworks' with exotic, curled petals. The display will last all summer.

Planting & care Plant the pot in late spring, when all risk of frost has passed, using a free-draining potting mix. Apply a liquid fertilizer every two weeks, and deadhead regularly, to encourage a succession of blooms. As the risk of frost approaches in the fall, transfer the heuchera to the garden. If you want to save the pelargoniums for next year, plant them in individual pots of free-draining potting mix and keep on a sunny windowsill indoors. Cut back hard in spring and use in next year's display pots.

Or you could try going for a softer look by replacing the dark, bold heuchera with light, frilly, silver-leaved thyme (*Thymus vulgaris* 'Silver Posie') and using a white or soft pink nemesia.

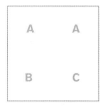

scent of summer

You need

4 *Nicotiana* cultivar (tobacco plant) **A**

8 purple *Viola* (pansy) **B**

8 cream *Viola* (pansy) **C**

8 *Lobelia erinus* cultivar **D**

Beautiful tobacco plants, with their exotic, heady scent, make great subjects for pots near the house. Here, they are combined with dusky purple and cream pansies and lobelias, making a gorgeous display for a shady spot.

Planting & care Plant the pot in late spring, when all risk of frost has passed, using a moisture-retentive, free-draining potting mix. Be sure to choose scented tobacco plants (not all of them are) and neat edging lobelia rather than the trailing type. Remove the flowers as they fade, to encourage the plants to produce more, and apply a liquid fertilize every two weeks.

Or you could try heliotrope (*Heliotropium arborescens*), another scented plant with lovely, purple flowers. Also known as cherry pie, the plant has an intoxicating, sweet scent. Use in the pot instead of the tobacco plants and place in full sun.

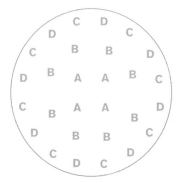

fantasy foliage

You need

2 *Pelargonium* cultivar
(fancy-leaved geranium) **A**

2 *Solenostemon* cultivar
(coleus) **B**

2 *Phormium tenax* cultivar
(New Zealand flax) **C**

1 *Chamaecyparis pisifera*
'Filifera' **D**

2 *Plectranthus forsteri*
'Marginatus' **E**

2 *Hypoestes* cultivar
(polka-dot plant) **F**

2 *Iresine herbstii* cultivar **G**

2 *Helichrysum petiolare*
'Limelight' **H**

2 *Hedera helix* cultivar (ivy) **I**

A rich mixture of colors, this eye-catching window box proves that foliage can be just as colorful as flowers. The display features plants of a wide range of habits—spiky, bushy, trailing—with curls and stripes for added interest.

Planting & care Plant the window box in late spring, when all risk of frost has passed, using a free-draining, moisture-retentive potting mix. Insert fertilizer pellets designed for foliage plants into the potting mix, to do the fertilizing for you. Keep the potting mix moist—there are a lot of plants packed in. At the end of the season, transfer the hardy phormium and chamaecyparis to the garden.

Or you could try a pink, purple, and silver display with pink-leaved *Phormium* 'Dazzler', a purple-leaved coleus such as 'Palisandra', silver helichrysum and *Plectranthus argentatus*, and a pink-and-cream-leaved pelargonium, such as 'Miss Burdett Coutts'.

purple haze

You need

3 *Salvia farinacea* (mealycup sage) **A**

8 *Petunia* cultivar **B**

6 *Isotoma axillaris* (laurentia) **C**

8 *Lobelia erinus* 'String of Pearls' **D**

A haze of purple flowers adorns a simple, white bowl in a display reminiscent of a summer meadow. There is starlike laurentia, blousy petunias in dark and pale purple, lobelias around the edges, and spikes of salvia in the center.

Planting & care Plant the pot in late spring, when all risk of frost has passed, using a free-draining potting mix. Apply a liquid fertilizer every two weeks, and deadhead regularly, to encourage the plants to produce further blooms.

Or you could try extending the meadow theme further and including some annual grasses, such as big quaking grass (*Briza maxima*), which looks a little like oats, or hare's tail (*Lagurus ovatus*), which has soft, fluffy heads tinged with purple.

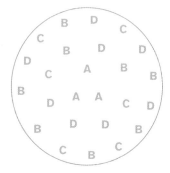

silver service

You need

2 *Dianthus* cultivar (pinks) **A**

2 *Euonymus fortunei*
cultivar (wintercreeper) **B**

1 *Convolvulus cneorum* **C**

The soft, silvery leaves of this evergreen
convolvulus make a fine foil for many other
container plants. Here they are teamed with an
evergreen spindle with cream-and-green foliage,
and pretty pinks with mounds of silver foliage
and scented pink flowers.

Planting & care Plant the container at any time of year,
using a free-draining potting mix, and topdress with a
layer of grit or fine gravel. Sprinkle a little bonemeal or
other slow-release fertilizer into the top of the container
each year in spring. Cut back the shrubs if necessary, to
keep tidy, and deadhead the pinks as they fade.

Or you could try a white-and-silver plant display using
Euonymus fortunei 'Emerald Gaiety', which has green-
and-white leaves, and a white-flowered pink, such as the
old-fashioned *Dianthus* 'Mrs Sinkins', 'Haytor White', or
'Musgrave's Pink', all of which have scented flowers.

shade lovers

You need

1 *Matteuccia struthiopteris*
(ostrich fern) **A**

1 *Alchemilla mollis*
(lady's mantle) **B**

1 *Tolmiea menziesii* 'Taff's
Gold' (piggyback plant) **C**

1 *Hosta* cultivar **D**

Colors are clearer in the shade, and this study in green benefits from lower light levels, where the subtleties of color can be really appreciated. Lime-greens and blue-greens mingle to create a gentle harmony.

Planting & care Plant the pot at any time of year, using a moisture-retentive potting mix to which you have added some well-rotted compost or manure. Keep the potting mix moist at all times and fork a little bonemeal or other slow-release fertilizer into the top of the potting mix each spring. These plants are herbaceous and will die down over winter, so remove the dead foliage in the fall or spring, ready for the new spring growth.

Or you could try other shade-loving perennials, such as rodgersia with its large, rhubarblike leaves, deadnettles (*Lamium*) with foliage in shades of silver, green, or yellow, or barrenwort (*Epimedium*) with lovely, heart-shaped, mottled leaves on thin, wiry stems.

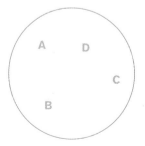

hanging gardens

You need

4 *Verbena* Tapien Series
'Purple' **A**

4 *Nemesia* Poetry
'Candyfloss' **B**

4 *Pelargonium* cultivar
(geranium) **C**

6 *Diascia* cultivar **D**

2 *Helichrysum petiolare*
'Limelight' **E**

2 *Brachyscome* cultivar
(Swan River daisy) **F**

6 *Lobelia* 'Waterfall Light
Lavender' **G**

This pretty hanging basket is a cascade of color, overflowing with all the favorite summer basket plants. Pelargoniums, verbenas, Swan River daisies, diascias, and nemesias mingle to create a glorious show.

Planting & care Plant the basket in late spring, when all risk of frost has passed, using a moisture-retentive potting mix to which you have added some moisture-retaining crystals. Insert some fertilizer pellets, as there are a lot of plants in a small amount of potting mix, and they'll need a regular supply of nutrients to flower well. Deadhead regularly through summer, to keep the flowers coming steadily.

Or you could try sticking to soft pastel shades and replacing the purple verbena with 'Tapien White' or 'Pink Parfait', and using pale pink pelargoniums.

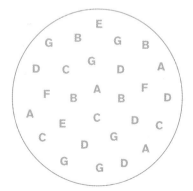

clematis creation

You need

1 *Clematis* 'Elsa Späth' **A**

1 *Clematis* 'Miss Bateman' **B**

1 *Clematis* 'Liberation' **C**

Gorgeous showy clematis, like these large-flowered cultivars, are ideal for container culture. The big, open blooms appear in early summer. Choose two or three cultivars that look good growing up together.

Planting & care Plant the pot at any time of year, using a moisture-retentive potting mix. Plant the clematis with their crowns around 3 in. (8 cm) below the surface of the soil, to protect against clematis wilt and encourage further stems to develop. Add a tepee to support them. Place in a sunny site with the pot in shade if possible, as these plants like cool roots. Cut back each of the stems to a pair of strong, healthy buds each year in early spring, and fork a little bonemeal or other slow-release fertilizer into the top of the potting mix.

Or you could try some of the other large-flowered clematis, such as 'Nelly Moser', a much-loved favorite with pink flowers with a dark stripe down each petal, or 'Beauty of Worcester' with double, blue flowers.

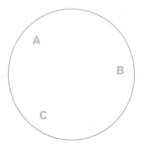

red, white, and blue

You need

5 *Verbena* Flamenco 'Dark Red' **A**

5 *Lobelia erinus* 'Blue Star' **B**

5 *Calibrachoa* Celebration 'White' **C**

A basic plastic hanging pot has been filled with three summer beauties in contrasting colors—red verbena, blue lobelia, and white calibrachoa—so full and healthy that the pot is no longer visible.

Planting & care Plant the hanging pot in late spring, when all risk of frost has passed, using a free-draining potting mix. Choose a pot with a built-in water reservoir if possible, to cut down on watering. Apply a liquid fertilizer every two weeks, and keep the potting mix just moist. Remove the growing tips of the verbena and calibrachoa as they grow, to encourage the plants to bush up.

Or you could try using blue daisies (*Felicia amelloides*) instead of the lobelia if you want a clearer blue. They are similar to Swan River daisies (*Brachyscome*), but the color is pure blue.

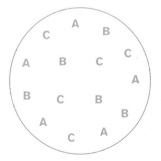

pansy perfection

You need

4 *Viola* cultivar (pansy;
   2 purple, 2 orange) **A**

4 *Viola* cultivar
   (smaller-flowered viola;
   2 purple, 2 yellow) **B**

3 *Argyranthemum* cultivar **C**

5 *Lobularia maritima*
   (sweet alyssum) **D**

4 *Hedera helix* cultivar (ivy) **E**

With all the other choices available, we often forget pansies for summer displays, yet they flower reliably right through the season. Here they are teamed up with white sweet alyssum, ivy, and argyranthemums in a window box.

Planting & care Plant in late spring, when all risk of frost has passed, using a moisture-retentive potting mix. Keep the mix just moist, and apply a liquid fertilizer every two weeks, to keep the flowers coming. Deadhead the argyranthemums, pansies, and violas regularly.

Or you could try combining brighter plants with the colorful pansies for a more eye-catching display. Try some of the tender foliage plants on offer for summer containers, such as coleus (*Solenostemon*), in vivid shades of crimson, purple, orange, and lime-green, or the lovely purple-leaved Persian shield (*Strobilanthes dyeriana*).

soft summer pinks

You need

4 *Pelargonium* cultivar
(geranium) **A**

3 *Fuchsia* cultivar **B**

2 *Diascia* cultivar **C**

2 *Nemesia* cultivar **D**

2 *Impatiens* cultivar (busy
Lizzie) **E**

2 *Petunia* 'Surfinia Rose
Vein' **F**

2 *Verbena* 'Tapien White' **G**

2 *Sutera* cultivar **H**

1 *Glechoma hederacea*
'Variegata' **I**

This soft, floriferous display of pastel pinks is the epitome of summer, with pelargoniums and fuchsias playing the leading role. Here the plants fill a window box, but they'd look just as good in a hanging basket or patio pot.

Planting & care Plant the window box in late spring, when all risk of frost has passed, using a moisture-retentive potting mix to which you have added some moisture-retaining crystals. Keep the mix just moist, and apply a liquid fertilizer every two weeks. Deadhead the plants regularly, to maintain a good show of flowers.

Or you could try other soft pink, summer flowers, such as osteospermum 'Arusha', pink lobelias, pale pink begonias, such as the double-flowered 'Pink Cloud', soft pink argyranthemums, such as 'Summit Pink' or the double-flowered 'Summersong Rose', or pale pink snapdragons (*Antirrhinum*).

a feast for the senses

You need

2 *Cosmos atrosanguineus*
(chocolate cosmos) **A**

2 *Solanum rantonnetii*
'Royal Robe' (blue potato
bush) **B**

2 *Pelargonium* 'Royal Oak'
(scented geranium) **C**

4 *Calibrachoa* cultivar **D**

This lovely collection of tender perennials is not just easy on the eye but on the nose too. Chocolate cosmos, with its chocolate-scented flowers, sits alongside a pretty blue potato bush, with a heady perfume, and the spicy-scented pelargonium 'Royal Oak'.

Planting & care Plant the pot in late spring, when all risk of frost has passed, using a free-draining potting mix. The display is designed to be viewed from one side only, so the taller plants are arranged at the back. Keep the potting mix just moist, and apply a liquid fertilizer every two weeks or so through the summer. Deadhead regularly, to encourage a succession of flowers.

Or you could try a container with just scented pelargoniums of different types. 'Lady Plymouth' has pretty, cream-edged leaves with a eucalyptus scent, 'Mabel Grey' has a strong, lemon scent, while 'Graveolens' smells of roses. Place the container where you will brush past it and release the scent.

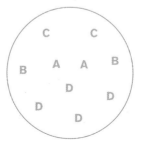

weird and wonderful

You need

1 *Ricinus communis* (castor bean) **A**

3 *Amaranthus caudatus* cultivar (love-lies-bleeding; 2 red, 1 green) **B**

1 *Aeonium* 'Zwartkop' **C**

1 *Brassica* cultivar (ornamental brassica) **D**

2 *Petunia* 'Mirage Midnight' **E**

1 *Pelargonium* cultivar (geranium) **F**

1 *Tradescantia pallida* 'Purpurea' **G**

This unusual display of deep reds, purples, and greens focuses on unusual foliage, with the large, showy leaves of a castor bean, a curly gray-green brassica, a purple-leaved tradescantia, and a black aeonium.

Planting & care Plant the container in late spring, when all risk of frost has passed, using a moisture-retentive potting mix. Keep the potting mix moist, and apply a liquid fertilizer every two weeks. Deadhead the flowers as they fade, to keep them coming. As the risk of frost approaches later in the year, transplant the aeonium, pelargonium, and tradescantia into small pots and enjoy them as houseplants on a sunny windowsill.

Or you could try the rich reds and purples of coleus (*Solenostemon*) instead of the amaranthus and brassica, to add more color.

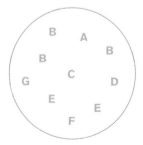

pink daisies

You need

1 *Pericallis* x *hybrida*
'Senetti Magenta Bi-color'
(cineraria) **A**

1 *Pericallis* x *hybrida*
Senetti Series 'Magenta'
(cineraria) **B**

2 *Argyranthemum* 'Summer
Melody' **C**

A muted gray pot is the perfect foil for a dazzling array of pink daisy flowers. Brilliantly bright cinerarias and softer pink argyranthemums are a wonderful combination for early summer before most summer bedding plants have started flowering.

Planting & care Plant the pot in late spring, when all risk of frost has passed. Although the cinerarias are fairly hardy, argyranthemums will be cut down by late frosts. Use a free-draining potting mix and keep it just moist. Apply a liquid fertilizer every two weeks, and deadhead regularly, to maintain a succession of flowers.

Or you could try deep blue-and-white cineraria 'Senetti Bi-color Blue' with a white argyranthemum, such as 'Summersong White' or 'Ping-Pong'.

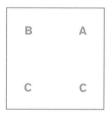

warm welcome

You need

1 *Argyranthemum* 'Jamaica Primrose' **A**

2 *Phygelius* cultivar (Cape figwort) **B**

2 *Molinia caerulea* subsp. *caerulea* 'Variegata' (variegated purple moor grass) **C**

2 *Ophiopogon planiscapus* 'Nigrescens' **D**

2 *Calibrachoa* cultivar **E**

4 *Peperomia* cultivar **F**

6 *Hedera helix* cultivar (ivy) **G**

A lovely combination of grasses and flowers in rich shades of russet and yellow offers a warm welcome on the doorstep. The color scheme has been designed to tie in with the yellow sandstone wall behind.

Planting & care Plant the pot in late spring, when all risk of frost has passed, using a free-draining potting mix. Keep the potting mix just moist, and apply a liquid fertilizer every two weeks. Deadhead regularly, to encourage more flowers to come.

Or you could try lightening the display, using a pale yellow phygelius, such as Candydrops Series 'Cream', and swapping the black ophiopogon and peperomia for Bowles's golden sedge (*Carex elata* 'Aurea') and a pale heuchera, such as 'Key Lime Pie'.

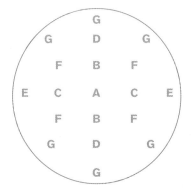

box of blooms

You need

3 *Pelargonium* Trend 'Lavender' **A**

2 *Petunia* 'Surfinia Purple Vein' **B**

2 *Brachyscome* cultivar (Swan River daisy) **C**

This window box, adorning a balcony rail, is packed with blooms, with geraniums, petunias, and Swan River daisies flowering extravagantly. Fertilize and deadhead regularly, to achieve such a magnificent display.

Planting & care Plant the window box in late spring, when all risk of frost has passed, using a moisture-retentive potting mix. Remove the growing tips of the plants when they are young, to encourage bushiness: this will delay flowering a little but increase the number of flowers produced. Apply a liquid fertilizer every week, and remove blooms as soon as they fade, to encourage more to be produced. Keep the mix just moist at all times.

Or you could try the same display in white, with pure white pelargonium 'Aphrodite', *Petunia* 'Surfinia Vanilla', and white Swan River daisies.

precious gems

You need

4 *Verbena* Romance 'Purple' **A**

4 *Begonia semperflorens*
cultivar **B**

2 *Helichrysum petiolare* **C**

An elegant, square, silver planter has been filled with verbenas, begonias, and silver helichysums arranged like gems in a jewelry box. Place on a dining table outdoors or on the top of a wall, where it can be appreciated at close quarters.

Planting & care Plant the container in late spring, when all risk of frost has passed, using a moisture-retentive potting mix. Tuck a little dried Spanish moss around the plants, to hide the potting mix. Remove the growing tips of the plants when they are young, to encourage bushiness. Water and fertilize regularly, and trim off any stray stems, to keep the plants neat.

Or you could try rich ruby-red begonias, which have a jewel-like quality, with scarlet or deep pink verbena. Be sure to choose a low-growing, compact verbena cultivar such as Romance 'Pink', or 'Red'.

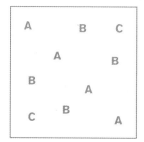

sweet scent

You need

10 *Lathyrus odoratus* 'Galaxy Mixed' (sweet pea) **A**

4 *Pelargonium* 'Flower Fairy Berry' (geranium) **B**

6 *Petunia* 'Purple Lady' **C**

6 *Pelargonium* (scented-leaved geranium) **D**

A tepee of twigs supports pretty, scented sweet peas in mixed colors, underplanted with pink petunias and pelargoniums, and a selection of scented-leaved pelargoniums.

Planting & care Plant the pot in late spring, when all risk of frost has passed. Sweet peas do best in a rich potting mix, so add plenty of well-rotted compost or manure to the base of the pot as you fill it with moisture-retentive potting mix. Apply a liquid fertilizer every two weeks, and deadhead all the plants regularly, to maintain a succession of flowers.

Or you could try the everlasting pea (*Lathyrus latifolius*), which is a hardy perennial vine. It comes up every year with pretty, blue-green foliage and rich pink flowers, so it can stay in the pot permanently.

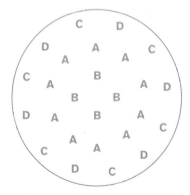

minimeadow

You need

4 *Jasione laevis* (sheep's
bit) **A**

2 *Scabiosa* 'Pink Mist' (small
scabious) **B**

4 *Deschampsia flexuosa* 'Tatra
Gold' (crinkled hair grass) **C**

2 *Festuca glauca* 'Blaufuchs'
(blue fescue) **D**

A tin bathtub has been planted with a rather
glamorous version of a wildflower meadow. The
pretty, pink and lilac, nodding heads of sheep's
bit and small scabious are surrounded by
designer grasses in blue and green.

Planting & care Plant the tub at any time of year, using a
free-draining potting mix. First make sure there are plenty
of drainage holes in the base of the tub—if not, make
some with a drill. Keep the potting mix just moist, and
fork a little bonemeal or other slow-release fertilizer into
the top of the potting mix each spring.

Or you could try including diminutive alpine poppies
(*Papaver alpinum*) in the tub, to extend the meadow
theme. These sweet, little perennials come in pretty
shades of white, pink, yellow, and orange and should
self-sow to produce different colors each year.

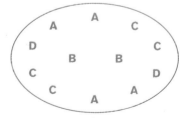

regal roses

You need

4 *Rosa* 'Ruby Anniversary'
  (rose) **A**

A handsome, wooden planter, colored with scarlet woodstain, is home to a group of rich red patio rose 'Ruby Anniversary'. If deadheaded, the roses will provide many weeks of vivid color throughout summer.

Planting & care Plant the roses at any time of year in a moisture-retentive, free-draining potting mix to which you have added some well-rotted compost or manure. Fork a little bonemeal or other slow-release fertilizer into the top of the potting mix each spring, and mulch with more well-rotted compost or manure. Prune the roses in late fall.

Or you could try staining a wooden planter with lilac or blue woodstain, and planting with the floribunda (cluster-flowered) rose 'Shocking Blue', which has pretty, fragrant, lilac-purple flowers.

perfumed perfection

You need

3 *Matthiola incana* (stocks) **A**

5 *Viola* cultivar (smaller-
flowered viola) **B**

Pure white stocks and soft mauve violas in a galvanized container make an effective display against the rich blue background of the shed behind. The stocks have a wonderful perfume, so place the pot on a table close to nose level.

Planting & care Plant the pot in late spring, when all risk of frost has passed, using a free-draining, moisture-retentive potting mix. Fertilize every two weeks with a liquid fertilizer, and deadhead the flowers regularly, to prolong the display.

Or you could try using night-scented stocks (*Matthiola longipetala* subsp. *bicornis*), which have smaller flowers in white and shades of pink or mauve but the most magnificent perfume in the evenings. Place the container on the table on the patio for those warm, summer evenings under the stars.

snappy show

You need

2 *Antirrhinum majus* 'Bells Red' (trumpet-flowered snapdragon) **A**

2 *Antirrhinum majus* Tahiti 'Pink and White' (snapdragon) **B**

4 *Solenostemon* 'Wizard' (coleus) **C**

2 *Hedera helix* cultivar (ivy) **D**

Cheerful snapdragons fill a rustic wooden planter with vibrant, chocolate-and-lime coleus and ivies to soften the edges. Choose a range of snapdragons with different flower shapes, including trumpet-flowered, azalea-flowered, and traditional snaps.

Planting & care Plant the container in late spring, when all risk of frost has passed, using a moisture-retentive potting mix. Keep the mix just moist and fertilize every two weeks with a liquid fertilizer. Deadhead the snapdragons regularly, to prolong the flowering period.

Or you could try snapdragon 'Black Prince' with the chocolate-and-lime coleus. The foliage is bronze, and the flowers are a wonderful, velvety dark red. Team up with lime-green *Helichrysum petiolare* 'Limelight' around the edges of the pot, instead of the ivy.

dainty daisies

You need

1 *Felicia amelloides* (blue daisy) **A**

2 *Brachyscome* cultivar (Swan River daisy) **B**

A handsome, ceramic wall pot is home to a simple combination of daisies, both Swan River daisies in lilac and blue daisies in clear blue, forming a soft mound of fine foliage topped with a profusion of dainty flowers.

Planting & care Plant the pot in late spring, when all risk of frost has passed, using a moisture-retentive potting mix. Because the pot doesn't hold much soil and will dry out quickly, add some moisture-retaining crystals to the potting mix. Water daily, and fertilize every two weeks with a liquid fertilizer. Deadhead regularly, to maintain a succession of flowers.

Or you could try combining the variegated blue daisy (*Felicia amoena* 'Variegata'), with its bright cream-edged foliage, with a white Swan River daisy, such as *Brachyscome* 'White Splendor'.

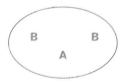

purple fountain

A gorgeous, purple fountain grass makes a graceful centerpiece for a white, wooden planter. It is surrounded by blue fairy fan-flowers for a pleasing contrast of color and form.

You need

1 *Pennisetum setaceum* 'Rubrum' (fountain grass) **A**

4 *Scaevola aemula* (fairy fan-flower) **B**

Planting & care Plant the pot in late spring, when all risk of frost has passed, using a moisture-retentive potting mix. Keep the mix moist, and apply a liquid fertilizer every two weeks. The fountain grass is perennial and hardy in zone 9, where you may get it to survive in the pot over winter by cutting off all the foliage in late fall and wrapping the container in bubble wrap to protect it from frost. Unwrap in midspring, and keep your fingers crossed for emerging foliage soon afterwards.

Or you could try one of the pink pennisetums, such as *Pennisetum glaucum* 'Jester' with rich pink, burgundy, and bronze tones to its foliage. Team up with deep pink Surfinia petunias for a colorful show.

fancy fuchsias

You need

3 *Fuchsia* 'Garden News' **A**

4 *Verbena* 'Sissinghurst' **B**

2 *Scaevola aemula* (fairy fan-flower) **C**

Blousy, pink fuchsias, deep pink verbena, and rich blue fairy fan-flowers mingle together in a lovely, aged, terra-cotta bowl. The bowl, with its strong lines, lends itself to a soft and full planting with trailing stems and lots of flowers.

Planting & care Plant the bowl in late spring, when all risk of frost has passed, using a moisture-retentive potting mix. This bowl will dry out quickly, so it is a good idea to line it with plastic to retain moisture. Be sure to make some holes in the plastic in the base of the bowl. Water regularly, and fertilize every two weeks with a liquid fertilizer. Remove the blooms as they fade, to encourage more to come. This fuchsia is hardy in zone 8, where it can be transferred to the garden in the fall.

Or you could try some of the other lovely fuchsias on offer, such as the unusually colored 'Amazing Maisie' with pink and orange flowers, teamed up with pink and orange *Lantana camara* around the edges of the bowl.

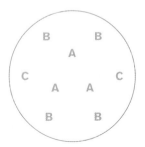

exotic beauties

You need

2 *Fuchsia* 'Thalia' **A**

3 *Bidens ferulifolia* **B**

3 *Pelargonium* cultivar
(ivy-leaved pelargonium) **C**

2 *Lotus berthelotii* **D**

1 *Tropaeolum* cultivar
(nasturtium) **E**

1 *Salvia discolor* **F**

A full and varied display of foliage and flowers is given an exotic feel by the dark, dusky leaves of fuchsia 'Thalia' and the strange, black flowers of an unusual, tender salvia.

Planting & care Be sure to choose a tall pot to allow the trailing plants plenty of space to hang. Plant the container in late spring, when all risk of frost has passed, using a moisture-retentive potting mix. Fertilize every two weeks with a liquid fertilizer, and keep deadheading, to maintain the display right through summer. The lotus will go on to produce bright red, claw-shaped flowers on its gray, ferny foliage.

Or you could try leaving out the yellow bidens and replacing it with vivid scarlet *Lantana camara* instead, for an even more dramatic effect.

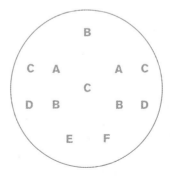

little gem

You need

1 *Lobelia erinus* cultivar **A**

A dainty, wicker basket on a simple, metal chain has been planted with a single, sapphire-blue lobelia. Usually used as a filler, lobelia can hold its own as the star attraction.

Planting & care Plant the basket in late spring, when all risk of frost has passed. First line the basket with plastic, to retain moisture and hold the potting mix in place, then make a few drainage holes in the plastic, to allow excess water to drain away. Fill the basket with moisture-retentive potting mix to which you have added some moisture-retaining crystals. Fertilize every two weeks with a liquid fertilizer, to prolong the flowering period, and water regularly to keep the potting mix moist.

Or you could try filling a number of identical baskets with lobelias in different shades of blue. Hang the baskets from a pergola over a seating area or from the branches of a tree close to the patio.

dizzy daisies

You need

1 *Lasthenia glabrata* **A**

3 *Calendula officinalis*
  (pot marigold) **B**

5 *Viola* cultivar (pansy) **C**

3 *Bellis perennis* cultivar
  (English daisy) **D**

A white, wooden planter has been filled with pansy and daisy flowers. A profusion of yellow lasthenia flowers rises above the chunky blooms of white English daisies and yellow pot marigolds. Deep red pansies add a richer contrast of color.

Planting & care Plant in late spring, when all risk of frost has passed, using a free-draining potting mix. Apply a liquid fertilizer every two weeks, and deadhead regularly, to maintain a show of flowers. Although the lasthenia is an annual, cut it back when it becomes leggy and bears fewer flowers, and it should grow again, to produce a second flush of blooms.

Or you could try *Bidens ferulifolia* for a similar effect if you can't find *Lasthenia glabrata*. The foliage has a softer, more ferny appearance but the flowers are a close match.

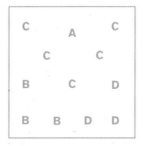

dark and mysterious

You need

2 *Lagurus ovatus*
(hare's tail) **A**

3 *Begonia rex* cultivar **B**

2 *Tradescantia zebrina*
(wandering jew) **C**

2 *Viola* 'Blackjack' (pansy) **D**

Sumptuous, fancy-leaved begonias in shades of black, gray, and pink are offset by gray-striped tradescantia, the fluffy heads of hare's tail, and jet-black pansies—an eye-catching show for a shady spot in summer.

Planting & care Plant the trough in late spring, when all risk of frost has passed, using a moisture-retentive potting mix. Keep the potting mix just moist, and fertilize from time to time with a liquid fertilizer. Remove the flowers from the pansies as they fade, to encourage more blooms. At the end of the season, as the risk of frost approaches, transplant the begonias and tradescantias into individual pots and bring indoors as houseplants. Discard the annual hare's tail and pansies.

Or you could try other black flowers, such as fuchsia 'Roesse Blacky', pelargonium 'Black Rose', the black lily 'Landini', or the black arum *Zantedeschia* 'Black Forest' with its sinister, cone-shaped flowers.

essence of summer

You need

1 *Argyranthemum* cultivar **A**

1 *Verbena* Tapien Pink **B**

6 *Pelargonium* 'Belle Ville Mixed' (geranium) **C**

2 *Helichrysum petiolare* **D**

1 *Fuchsia* cultivar **E**

A pretty, blue-leaved argyranthemum forms a cloud of fine foliage and white flowers in a white, wooden planter. It is underplanted with bright pink, trailing geraniums, verbena, soft pink fuchsias, and silver helichrysum, the essence of summer containers.

Planting & care Plant the pot in late spring, when all risk of frost has passed, using a free-draining potting mix. Remove the growing tips of the plants when small, to encourage bushiness, and keep the potting mix just moist. Apply a liquid fertilizer every two weeks, and deadhead all the plants regularly, to maintain a show of flowers all season long.

Or you could try a pure white display with verbena Tapien White, pelargonium 'Belle Ville White', and the lovely fuchsia 'Hawkshead'.

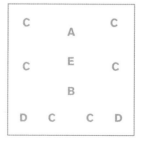

fall beauties

cool cabbages

You need

3 ornamental cabbages **A**

3 *Viola* cultivar (pansy) **B**

2 *Euonymus fortunei* 'Emerald Gaiety' **C**

2 *Calluna vulgaris* cultivar (Scotch heather) **D**

This cool fall design of greens and whites features the frilly heads of ornamental cabbages with pansies, heathers, and the striking foliage of euonymus in a simple, terra-cotta bowl.

Planting & care Plant the bowl in late summer, using a moisture-retentive potting mix. Keep moist and remove the pansy flowers as they fade, to encourage more to appear. When the cabbages and pansies are past their best, discard them and replace with fresh pansies and cabbages, to extend the display through to spring.

Or you could try pink ornamental cabbages with pink heathers and pale pink or white pansies.

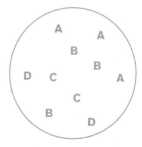

rich fall pinks

You need

3 *Calluna vulgaris* cultivar
(Scotch heather; 2 white,
1 pink) **A**

3 *Viola* cultivar (pansy) **B**

A simple collection of heathers and pansies in
white and rich pink fills a woven-twig wall basket
in the fall. The color scheme has been chosen to
complement the blue-stained shed on which the
basket is hanging.

Planting & care Plant the basket in late summer, using
a moisture-retentive, acidic-soil mix. Arrange two white
heathers at the back of the basket, one on either side,
and the pink heather in front and between the two. Pop
the pansies along the front of the basket, firm, and water
well. Water regularly, especially if the basket is hanging
in a warm, sunny place. When the plants finish flowering,
discard the pansies and plant the heathers in the garden.

Or you could try using fall-flowering gentians (*Gentiana
sino-ornata*) instead of the pansies. They have vivid blue,
trumpet flowers (perfect with a blue background) and
mossy green foliage. They are perennial plants, so
transfer them to the garden when they finish flowering.
Team them with white heathers.

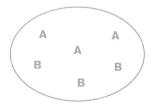

vegetable basket

You need

4 ornamental cabbages **A**

6 *Calluna vulgaris*
cultivar (Scotch heather) **B**

3 *Hedera helix* cultivar (ivy) **C**

A simple, wire hanging basket has been lined with conifer foliage and filled with pretty, pink cabbages, heathers, and ivies for a soft and appealing fall display.

Planting & care Plant the basket in late summer. Start by lining the empty basket with conifer foliage, to hold the potting mix in place. The foliage will gradually turn an attractive russet-brown. Fill the basket with moisture-retentive, acidic-soil mix, and arrange the plants in the top. Plant the central cabbage a little higher than the others, to make it more visible. Keep the soil moist, especially if the basket is hanging in a warm, sunny place. When the plants have finished flowering, discard the cabbages and plant the heathers in the garden. The ivies can be kept in the basket for a winter display.

Or you could try replacing the cabbages with pale pink osteospermums, with their big, bold daisy flowers. They start flowering in late spring or early summer, but will still be going strong in the fall.

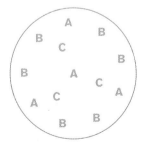

fiery glow

You need

1 *Physalis alkekengi* (Chinese lantern) **A**

2 orange chrysanthemums **B**

1 *Lysimachia nummularia* (creeping Jenny) **C**

1 *Ajania pacifica* 'Desert Flame' **D**

1 *Carex oshimensis* 'Evergold' (sedge) **E**

1 *Sedum* 'Lemon Ball' (stonecrop) **F**

This stunning display of Chinese lanterns and bright orange chrysanthemums fills a window box with fiery fall colors. The window box has been painted pale yellow, to set off the color of the plants magnificently.

Planting & care Plant the window box in late summer, using a moisture-retentive potting mix. Choose bushy chrysanthemum plants with plenty of buds. Place the display in a sheltered spot, and keep the potting mix just moist. Remove the chrysanthemum flowers as they fade. Although all the plants are perennials, this is only a temporary display as there are too many plants in such a small space. Transfer the plants to the garden after flowering, and replace with a winter-interest display.

Or you could try bright yellow chrysanthemums for an all-gold display. Use three chrysanthemum plants, and leave out the Chinese lanterns.

winter winners

winter wonders

You need

5 *Cyclamen* **A**

6 *Viola* cultivar (purple bedding violas) **B**

A colorful window box can brighten up even the dullest of winter days. Cheerful cyclamen in red, pink, and white are underplanted with purple violas in a pretty, late-winter display for a sheltered spot.

Planting & care Plant the window box in early to midwinter, using a free-draining potting mix. Make sure the cyclamen are hardy plants that have been bred to grow outsidein your region. Place the window box in a sheltered spot where it will be protected from the worst of the winter wet. Water sparingly to keep the potting mix just moist. Discard the plants when they have finished flowering in spring.

Or you could try a more formal mixture of all-red cyclamen and white violas. Add some variegated ivy to trail over the front of the box.

advanced guard

You need

20 early-flowering species
   crocus bulbs, such as
   Crocus ancyrensis or
   C. reticulatus **A**

15 *Iris reticulata* bulbs **B**

The warmth of the wall on which this terra-cotta pot is fixed will advance the flowering period of these sweet, little crocuses and irises and bring them into flower in late winter—a little taste of the spring to come.

Planting & care Plant up the pot in the fall, using a free-draining potting mix. Fill to within 3 in. (8 cm) of the rim of the pot, and arrange the bulbs on top of the mix, pointed ends uppermost. Add another 2 in. (5 cm) of potting mix, and firm lightly. Hang the pot on a sunny, sheltered wall, and keep the potting mix just moist over winter. Fertilize with a liquid fertilizer after the bulbs have finished flowering, or plant them out in the garden instead and use the pot for summer bedding.

Or you could try growing snowdrops (*Galanthus*) and winter aconites (*Eranthis*) in the pot, both of which naturally flower in late winter, for a cheerful, yellow and white display.

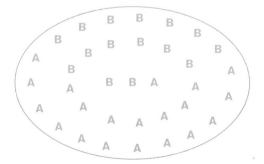

greens and creams

You need

1 *Hebe* 'Silver Queen' **A**

3 *Carex conica* 'Snowline' (sedge) **B**

3 *Carex pilulifera* 'Tinney's Princess' (sedge) **C**

6 *Hedera helix* cultivar (ivy) **D**

This pleasingly curvy, terra-cotta pot contains a selection of evergreen foliage in shades of cream and green: pretty variegated ivies, stripy sedges, and a bushy hebe in the center, which will produce lovely, pinky-purple flowers from mid- to late summer.

Planting & care Plant the pot at any time of year, using a free-draining potting mix. Keep the mix moist, and fork a little bonemeal or other slow-release fertilizer into the top of the potting mix each year in spring. Remove the hebe flowers as they fade, and trim the ivies if they become straggly.

Or you could try growing *Hebe* 'Autumn Glory', which has bronze shoots, red-edged leaves, and lovely, purple-blue flowers from midsummer right through fall. Combine it with one of the brown-leaved sedges, such as *Carex petriei* or *C. comans*.

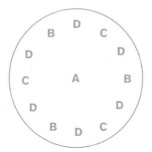

precious metals

You need

1 *Phormium tenax* 'Bronze'
(New Zealand flax) **A**

1 *Heuchera* 'Pewter Moon'
(coral flower) **B**

1 *Erica carnea* cultivar (winter
heath) **C**

This stylish, metallic pot contains spiky, bronze New Zealand flax and pewter-leaved coral flower, with a rich pink heath to brighten the planting—a handsome and sophisticated display for the dull, winter months.

Planting & care Plant the pot at any time of year, using a free-draining potting mix. Keep the potting mix moist, and fork a little bonemeal or other slow-release fertilizer into the top of the soil each year in spring. All the plants are evergreen, so the container will look good year-round, although the display will come to life when the heath blooms in winter.

Or you could try growing the plants in a galvanized metal container, such as a large bucket, trough, or trashcan. Don't forget to make plenty of drainage holes in the base of the container if it hasn't been designed with plants in mind.

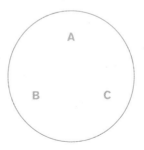

evergreen elegance

You need

1 *Viburnum tinus*
(laurustinus) **A**

2 *Skimmia japonica*
cultivar **B**

2 *Gaultheria procumbens*
(checkerberry) **C**

2 *Heuchera* cultivar (coral
flower) **D**

10 *Hedera helix* cultivar
(ivy) **E**

This window box is overflowing with handsome,
evergreen foliage, elegant, winter flowers, and
berries. The lovely, scented laurustinus flowers
will be replaced by black berries as the season
progresses, while the smart, red skimmia buds
will open into full, white blooms.

Planting & care Plant the window box in the fall, using
a moisture-retentive potting mix. Keep the mix moist by
regular watering, if the box is sheltered from the rain.
Fork a little bonemeal or other slow-release fertilizer
into the top of the potting mix each year in spring.

Or you could try creating a formal, green-and-white
display using gorgeously scented, white-flowered
Christmas box (*Sarcococca confusa*), instead of the
skimmias, and *Gaultheria mucronata* 'Wintertime' with
its bright white berries. Replace the bronze-leaved coral
flower with *Heuchera* 'Snow Storm', which has green
leaves with white marbling.

jolly jumble

You need

1 *Erica carnea* cultivar (winter heath) **A**

2 *Juniperus* cultivar (juniper) **B**

2 *Senecio cineraria* (cineraria) **C**

2 *Vinca major* 'Variegata' (periwinkle) **D**

4 *Cyclamen* **E**

1 *Solanum pseudocapsicum* (winter cherry) **F**

1 *Viola* cultivar (pansy) **G**

3 *Hedera helix* cultivar (ivy) **H**

A plain, terra-cotta pot has been planted with a jumble of foliage, fruits, and flowers for late winter. This cheerful display features a wide range of colors, textures, and forms and needs to be placed in a sheltered place.

Planting & care Plant the pot in the fall, using a free-draining potting mix. The display is designed to be viewed from one side only, so the taller plants are arranged at the back and the shorter plants at the front. Stand the pot in front of a wall, hedge, or fence in a sunny spot, sheltered from wind, rain, and frosts.

Or you could try creating a similar display with tougher plants that can withstand colder weather. Leave out the cineraria, cyclamen, and winter cherry and replace them with silvery *Artemisia arborescens*, *Gaultheria mucronata* 'Cherry Ripe', with its red berries, and pale pink pansies.

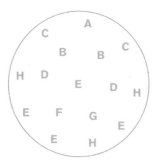

frosted berries

You need

1 *Skimmia japonica*
  subsp. *reevesiana* **A**

3 *Euonymus fortunei*
  'Emerald 'n' Gold'
  (wintercreeper) **B**

3 *Hedera helix* cultivar (ivy) **C**

6 *Tiarella cordifolia* (foam
  flower) **D**

The plentiful, red berries of skimmia look especially lovely when dusted with frost. Here, they are combined with golden wintercreeper, variegated ivy, and foam flower in a terra-cotta-look, resin pot, making a colorful and vibrant display for a shady spot in the dull, winter months.

Planting & care Plant the pot at any time of year, using a free-draining, moisture-retentive potting mix. Stand in a shady spot, and keep the potting mix just moist. Fork a little bonemeal or other slow-release fertilizer into the top of the soil each spring. The skimmia will produce fragrant, white flowers in spring, while the foam flower throws up tall stems of foamy, white flowers in summer.

Or you could try a cool, all-white display using *Skimmia japonica* 'Fructo Albo', with its green, spring flowers and pretty, white berries.

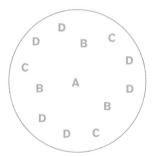

green tapestry

You need

1 *Skimmia* x *confusa* 'Kew Green' **A**

1 *Acorus gramineus* 'Ogon' (Japanese rush) **B**

1 *Leucothoe fontanesiana* 'Rainbow' **C**

1 *Lonicera nitida* 'Lemon Beauty' **D**

Four evergreen plants make an intricate tapestry with just their varied foliage to complete the picture: spiky, stripy rush, mottled leucothoe, the tiny, cream-edged leaves of lonicera, and bold, dark green skimmia, with the added bonus of its green flower buds.

Planting & care Plant the pot at any time of year, using a free-draining, moisture-retentive, acidic-soil mix. Fork a little bonemeal or other slow-release fertilizer into the soil mix in spring each year. The leucothoe will reward you with bell-shaped, white flowers in spring, while the green buds of the skimmia will open to wonderfully fragrant, white flowers.

Or you could try using other evergreen shrubs with interesting foliage, such as *Euonymus fortunei* cultivars, variegated or gray-leaved hebes, silvery *Convolvulus cneorum* or wormwood (*Artemisia*), or some of the yellow-splashed elaeagnus cultivars, such as *Elaeagnus* x *ebbingei* 'Limelight'.

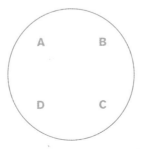

bare branches

With their architectural branches in shades of red, orange, and yellow, dogwoods are great for winter containers. Here the pinky stems of 'Cardinal' rise above a sea of white heath.

You need

2 *Cornus sericea* 'Cardinal' (red osier dogwood) **A**

3 *Erica carnea* 'Winter Snow' (winter heath) **B**

Planting & care Plant the container at any time of year, using a free-draining acidic-soil mix. Fork a little bonemeal or other slow-release fertilizer into the top of the soil mix each spring. To maintain a display of colored, bare wood each winter, cut back all the stems hard to within two or three buds of the base, in early spring. New stems will grow up through the spring and summer, ready to take on a lovely, pinky hue in winter. Place in full sun for the best color.

Or you could try a different color scheme: perhaps lovely, yellow-stemmed *Cornus sericea* 'Flaviramea' with *Erica carnea* 'Golden Starlet', with its lime-green foliage and white flowers; or brilliant red-stemmed *Cornus alba* 'Sibirica' with *Erica carnea* 'Myretoun Ruby' or 'December Red', both of which have deep pink-red flowers.

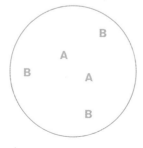

winter sunshine

You need

3 *Cyclamen* **A**

2 *Euonymus fortunei* 'Emerald 'n' Gold' (wintercreeper) **B**

1 ornamental chili pepper **C**

1 yellow *Solanum pseudocapsicum* (winter cherry) **D**

3 *Hedera helix* cultivar (ivy) **E**

A black window box is adorned with blousy, white cyclamen, golden, ornamental chili peppers, handsome, variegated foliage, and round winter cherry berries that will soon turn bright yellow.

Planting & care Plant the window box in the fall, using a free-draining potting mix. Stand it in a sheltered place, protected from winter winds, rain, and frost: this is perfect for a sunny, urban windowsill. Keep the potting mix just moist, and apply a liquid fertilizer about two months after planting. When the plants have finished their display, discard the cyclamen, pepper, and winter cherry but leave the wintercreepers and ivy in the window box, to act as a framework for a spring display.

Or you could try a scarlet design with bright red cyclamen, a red chili pepper, and a red winter cherry. Choose white-and-green ivies and *Euonymus fortunei* 'Emerald Gaiety', with its handsome, white-and-green foliage.

year-round

evergreen collection

This handsome collection of evergreen plants offers great variety in foliage color, shape, and habit, from trailing ivies to upright rushes, and from glossy pittosporum to fuzzy juniper.

You need

1 *Acorus gramineus* 'Ogon' (Japanese rush) **A**

1 dwarf *Juniperus* cultivar (juniper) **B**

1 *Pittosporum tenuifolium* cultivar **C**

2 *Hedera helix* cultivar (ivy) **D**

Planting & care Plant the container at any time of year, using a free-draining, moisture-retentive potting mix. Fork a little bonemeal or other slow-release fertilizer into the top of the potting mix each spring. Trim over the plants from time to time, to remove any dead foliage and keep them tidy. The pittosporum will reward you with honey-scented, bell-shaped flowers in late spring. Although the pittosporum is hardy in zone 9, it will do best in a sheltered site protected from hard frosts.

Or you could try growing these plants in a window box. Arrange two pittosporums and three junipers along the back of the box, evenly spaced; plant a Japanese rush at each end, and arrange six trailing ivies along the front.

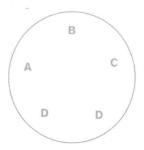

graceful grasses

You need

3 *Festuca* cultivars (fescue) **A**

A simple line of three grasses is the perfect foil for an elegant, gold-rimmed trough. The soft sage-green of the trough is picked up in the green grass foliage—a lovely harmonious centerpiece for an *alfresco* dining table.

Planting & care Plant the trough at any time of year, using a free-draining potting mix to which you have added some moisture-retaining crystals. Space the grasses evenly in the trough: symmetry is vital here. Firm the potting mix and add a topdressing of gravel, stone chips, grit, or colored ground glass mulch, to cover the potting mix and to add to the decorative appeal.

Or you could try painting a terra-cotta trough with soft blue, acrylic paint instead, and adding a silver rim using acrylic paint. Plant the painted trough with blue- or silver-leaved fescues, such as *Festuca glauca* 'Blaufuchs' or *F. valesiaca* 'Silbersee'.

tender succulents

You need

12 *Echeveria elegans* **A**

6 *Soleirolia soleirolii*
(Irish moss) **B**

1 *Aeonium* 'Zwartkop' **C**

Rosette-forming succulents are perfect for hanging baskets as they clothe the sides with handsome, fleshy foliage. Here, pretty, blue echeveria is teamed with black aeonium and underplanted with green Irish moss, to cover the basket as the echeverias grow.

Planting & care Plant the basket at any time of year, using a free-draining potting mix. Space the Irish moss and echeverias evenly around the sides of the basket, and plant the aeonium in the top. Hang the basket in a sunny, sheltered spot outside, but protect from cold weather in winter. These plants are tender and need to be kept above 50°F (10°C): a greenhouse or near a south-facing window indoors would be ideal.

Or you could try a similar effect using hardy houseleeks (*Sempervivum*), which can stay outdoors year-round in many regions. Choose a selection of different colors for a tapestry effect.

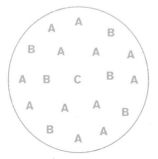

foliage and form

You need

1 *Hypericum* 'Magical Gold' **A**

1 *Acorus gramineus* 'Ogon' (Japanese rush) **B**

1 *Heuchera* 'Key Lime Pie' (coral flower) **C**

1 *Viola* cultivar (pansy) **D**

1 *Euonymus japonicus* 'Exstase' (Japanese spindle tree) **E**

A square, terra-cotta pot has been filled with a varied group of plants with interesting form and foliage in shades of greens and creams. The hypericum has aromatic foliage and produces fluffy, yellow flowers in summer, followed by cream-colored berries.

Planting & care Plant the pot at any time of year, using a moisture-retentive potting mix. Fork a little bonemeal or other slow-release fertilizer into the top of the soil mix in spring each year. As the pansy becomes too leggy and finishes flowering, replace it with a fresh plant. This is likely to be two or three times a year.

Or you could try a study in greens and whites with *Euonymus japonicus* 'Albomarginatus', a white pansy, *Heuchera* 'Schneewittchen', with its green leaves and white flowers, *Acorus gramineus* var. *pusillus* with its dark green leaves, and the white-and-green-leaved *Cornus alba* 'Elegantissima'.

bold bamboo

You need

1 *Pleioblastus* dwarf cultivar
(bamboo) **A**

4 x *Heucherella* cultivar **B**

This Japanese-style garden features a dwarf
bamboo in a handsome, black, glazed pot. The
rim of the pot is softened by the jagged foliage
of heucherella in a pleasing contrast with the
bamboo. A perfect, year-round display for sun
or partial shade.

Planting & care Plant the pot at any time of year, using
a moisture-retentive potting mix, and stand in sun or
partial shade. Fork a little bonemeal or other slow-release
fertilizer into the top of the soil mix each year in spring. To
keep the display neat, remove the tall heucherella flower
spikes when they appear in early summer.

Or you could try black bamboo (*Phyllostachys nigra*)
with its glossy, black canes, teamed up with a purple-
or pewter-leaved heuchera cultivar, such as *H. villosa*
'Palace Purple' or *H.* 'Pewter Moon'.

romantic topiary

You need

1 *Buxus microphylla* (small-
leaved boxwood) **A**

Topiary usually adds a formal note to a garden or patio area, but this pretty, boxwood heart is a little more relaxed in its approach. Buy a ready-trained plant for instant effect, or train one yourself if you have the patience.

Planting & care Keep the topiary on its own in a pot of free-draining potting mix, to maintain its foliage right down to soil level. Add a topdressing of grit, to smarten the appearance and to suppress weeds. The plant stems have to be trained on a rigid wire heart to form such a perfect shape. If you are training your own topiary, loosely bind the long, new shoots to the frame and trim off any other shoots that point in the wrong direction. To maintain a ready-trained topiary, keep the plant neat by trimming off new growths as they appear. Fork a little bonemeal or other slow-release fertilizer into the top of the potting mix each spring, and keep the soil just moist.

Or you could try other topiary shapes, such as simple cones or balls, or a series of clipped tiers with bare stems in between. If you train your own, your imagination is the only limiting factor.

heavenly hostas

You need

1 *Picea pungens* 'Globosa'
(Colorado spruce) **A**

1 *Euonymus japonicus*
'Ovatus Aureus' (Japanese
spindle tree) **B**

1 *Hosta* 'Wide Brim' **C**

Hostas make attractive container subjects,
spilling over the rim with their bold, heart-shaped
leaves. Here the colors of hosta 'Wide Brim' are
echoed in a soft blue, dwarf spruce and the
yellow variegation of a vibrant Japanese spindle.

Planting & care Plant the container at any time of year,
using a moisture-retentive potting mix to which you have
added some well-rotted compost or manure. Place in
partial shade—some sunshine will maintain the bright
foliage colors, but protect the hosta from the midday sun.
Keep the potting mix moist at all times, because hostas
will not tolerate drought. Fork a little bonemeal or other
slow-release fertilizer into the top of the potting mix
each spring.

Or you could try a blue-and-silver display with a blue-
leaved hosta such as 'Blue Moon' or 'Halcyon' and
silver-leaved oleaster (*Elaeagnus* 'Quicksilver') instead
of the spindle.

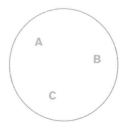

drought-busting basket

You need

1 *Aloe ferox* **A**

1 pink *Echeveria* cultivar **B**

4 *Echeveria elegans* cultivar **C**

2 *Sempervivum tectorum* (houseleek) **D**

1 *Rhodiola pachyclados* **E**

1 *Aeonium* 'Zwartkop' **F**

1 *Graptopetalum* cultivar **G**

Succulents are perfect for hanging baskets, because they are tolerant of drought, and it is notoriously difficult to keep potting mix moist in baskets. Choose a varied selection of different shapes and forms for a fascinating display.

Planting & care Plant the hanging basket at any time of year. Line the wire basket with burlap, and fill it with free-draining potting mix. Plant the succulents in the top and sides of the basket, aiming for a good contrast of shapes and colors. Hang the basket in a sunny, sheltered spot, and water from time to time in warm weather. These plants are tender and must be kept at a minimum of 50°F (10°C), so place in a greenhouse or in a sunny window indoors over winter.

Or you could try growing holiday cacti (*Schlumbergera*) in a hanging basket, as the spreading, fleshy stems hang down in an attractive manner. These tender plants produce prolific, vibrant pink and red flowers in late winter.

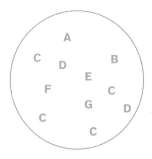

colorful cushions

You need

16 *Sempervivum* cultivars
(houseleek) **A**

A shallow bowl of gritty potting mix is the perfect place for a collection of houseleeks, which will form colorful cushions of neat rosettes. In summer, stems bearing clusters of exotic, little blooms appear above the rosettes.

Planting & care Plant the bowl at any time of year, using a free-draining potting mix to which you have added about a third by volume of grit or fine gravel. Place in a sunny spot, sheltered from heavy rain, and water only in very dry weather. Remove the old rosettes as they die after flowering, to be replaced by the new rosettes that form around the edges of the clumps. Apply a liquid fertilizer in spring each year.

Or you could try a collection of low-growing succulent stonecrops, such as *Sedum acre* with its fleshy, green stems and yellow flowers, *S. humifusum* with its hairy rosettes, *S. obtusatum* with its fat, red-tinged foliage, and *S. spathulifolium* 'Purpureum' with its fleshy rosettes in purple and gray.

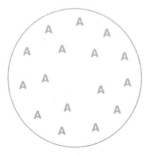

stripy sedges

You need

1 *Anemanthele lessoniana* (pheasant's tail grass) **A**

3 *Carex ornithopoda* 'Variegata' (bird's foot sedge) **B**

3 *Heuchera villosa* 'Palace Purple' (coral flower) **C**

These tall, elegant, terra-cotta pots have been filled with grasses and coral flower in a naturalistic planting in muted shades. The plants enhance the honey-colored stone wall beside which the pots are standing.

Planting & care Plant the pots at any time of year, using a moisture-retentive potting mix. Tidy the grasses from time to time, by removing any dead stems. Keep the soil moist at all times and fork a little bonemeal or other slow-release fertilizer into the top of the mix each spring.

Or you could try planting a lime-green Bowles's golden sedge (*Carex elata* 'Aurea') in the center of the pot and foam flower (*Tiarella cordifolia*), instead of the purple-leaved coral flower, which is similar in form but has pale green leaves.

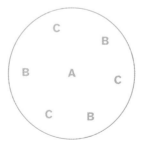

easy and edible

veg in vogue

You need

4 *Pelargonium* 'Lady Plymouth' **A**

4 *Mentha* x *piperita* (peppermint) **B**

4 spinach **C**

Who said the vegetable garden has to be hidden away? This cool and contemporary, galvanized planter boasts an elegant mixture of leafy spinach, upright peppermint, and frilly-leaved, eucalyptus-scented pelargoniums, which will perfume the air as you brush past.

Planting & care Plant the planter in spring, after all risk of frost has passed. Buy the mint and pelargoniums as young plants; spinach can be grown from seed sown *in situ*. Choose a fertile, moisture-retentive potting mix and keep it moist, to keep the spinach in growth: if the soil dries out, the spinach will go to seed. Harvest the spinach and mint as you need them, picking the outer spinach leaves first. Sow more spinach as necessary.

Or you could try growing New Zealand spinach instead. Although the flavor is not quite as good, it is easier to grow, more tolerant of windy or exposed sites and will not go to seed. Sow the seed in midspring, and start picking as soon as it is large enough.

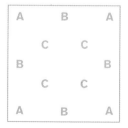

mediterranean flavors

You need

1 *Santolina chamaecyparissus* (lavender cotton) **A**

1 *Salvia officinalis* 'Purpurascens' (purple sage) **B**

1 *Salvia officinalis* (common sage) **C**

2 scented pelargoniums **D**

2 *Thymus vulgaris* (thyme) **E**

1 *Rosmarinus officinalis* (rosemary) **F**

A white-washed, terra-cotta pot is the perfect foil for a range of Mediterranean herbs, which look as good as they taste. Most of these plants are evergreen, so you can appreciate their decorative and culinary qualities right through the year.

Planting & care Plant the pot in spring, when all risk of frost has passed. Choose a free-draining potting mix and add a little extra grit, to improve the drainage even more. Remove the spent blooms from the lavender cotton and sage after flowering. The pelargoniums will die off over winter: remove the plants and replace them with new ones in spring.

Or you could try other Mediterranean herbs, such as fennel, with its feathery foliage and aniseed taste, lemon verbena, with its wonderful, lemony aroma, or lavender, with its beautiful, purple flowers.

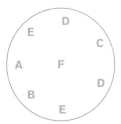

cool kale

You need

4 kale 'Nero di Toscana' **A**

9 *Allium schoenoprasum*
(chives) **B**

It's no surprise that kale is coming back into fashion: these handsome, architectural plants are extremely tough and hardy, producing a steady crop of succulent leaves from winter through to spring. Here they are underplanted with chives, another culinary staple.

Planting & care Plant the pot in late spring or summer, choosing a free-draining potting mix. Be sure to firm the potting mix well around the roots of the plants. Harvest the chives as you need them, but wait to start harvesting the kale until after the first frosts, as the flavor will be better. Choose only the tender, young leaves, because older leaves will be bitter. Replace the kale with fresh plants each spring or summer.

Or you could try some of the other kale cultivars, such as 'Red Russian' with its feathery, red leaves, 'Ragged Jack' with its pink-tinged foliage, or 'Redbor', a red, curly kale. All are just as attractive.

abundant aromatics

This simple, white window box is overflowing with herbs of all types. Place it on the kitchen windowsill for a ready supply of aromatics, whatever you are cooking.

You need

3 alpine strawberries **A**

1 scented pelargonium **B**

1 French lavender **C**

3 yellow variegated sage **D**

1 *Glechoma hederacea* 'Variegata' **E**

2 lemon balm **F**

2 nasturtiums **G**

1 chamomile **H**

1 sweet cicely **I**

1 lemongrass **J**

1 white variegated sage **K**

1 French marigold **L**

1 *Nepeta nervosa* (catmint) **M**

1 purple basil **N**

1 chives **O**

1 fennel **P**

1 golden feverfew **Q**

Planting & care Plant the window box in spring, using a range of small herb plants. Use a moisture-retentive potting mix and add moisture-retaining crystals, to sustain so many plants in a small space. It is also a good idea to insert fertilizer pellets into the potting mix, to nourish the plants. Discard the plants when the annuals die and the herbaceous perennials die back in winter, and start again with fresh plants the following spring.

Or you could try devoting the window box to just your favorite herb, rather than a whole mixture. For example, you could grow a range of different basils, including lemon basil, lime basil, purple basil, Thai basil, and 'Sweet Genovese' with tender, sweet, green foliage.

C	D	J	O	D	P
B	F	H	I	F	A	N	Q
A	E	G	D	K	L	M	A	G

bountiful beans

You need

4 dwarf bush bean
  'Berrgold' **A**

4 looseleaf lettuce 'Lollo
  Rossa' **B**

This hanging basket display comprises delicious, stringless, yellow beans and frilly, red lettuces, as appealing to the eye as to the palate. Fertilize and water well, and both will reward you with a good supply of produce for much of the summer.

Planting & care Plant the hanging basket in late spring, when all risk of frost has passed. Choose a moisture-retentive potting mix and add moisture-retaining crystals, to prevent the soil from drying out. Water every day, twice in very warm weather, and fertilize once a week. Harvest the beans as they become large enough: the more you pick, the more the plants will produce. These are nonhearting lettuces, so you can pick individual leaves as you need them, and the plants will produce more.

Or you could try combining 'Purple Queen' beans, which have handsome, purple pods, with bright green lettuce 'Lollo Bionda' for an equally eye-catching display.

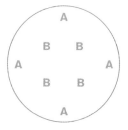

strawberry cocktail

You need

6 alpine strawberries **A**

2 *Borago officinalis* (borage) **B**

2 *Sanguisorba minor* (salad burnet) **C**

Tiny alpine strawberries and cucumber-scented borage are ideal for adding a refreshing taste to summer drinks and cocktails. Here they are planted in a galvanized bucket, together with salad burnet.

Planting & care Plant up the container in late spring, using a free-draining, moisture-retentive potting mix. Make sure there are plenty of drainage holes in the base of the bucket. Water regularly, and fertilize once a week, to encourage the strawberries to produce fruits. Pick the leaves and strawberries as you need them—they make a delicious and pretty decoration for summer desserts as well as cocktails. Discard the borage plants in winter, and replace with new plants in spring.

Or you could try using mint instead of borage, another favorite ingredient in summer drinks. Choose the pretty, variegated pineapple mint (*Mentha suaveolens* 'Variegata'), with its cream-and green-splashed leaves.

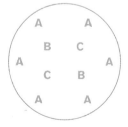

fish-lovers' favorites

You need

2 *Petroselinum crispum*
   (parsley) **A**

2 *Anethum graveolens*
   'Bouquet' (dill) **B**

1 *Artemisia dracunculus*
   (French tarragon) **C**

3 *Thymus citriodorus* 'Golden
   King' (lemon thyme) **D**

2 *Thymus vulgaris* 'Silver
   Posie' (thyme) **E**

This window-box display is designed for fish-lovers, with all the favorite herbs—parsley, dill, tarragon, and thyme—which enhance fish and seafood dishes. Use the leaves in sauces and marinades, or simply sprinkle over your fish on the barbecue.

Planting & care Plant the window box in spring, using a free-draining potting mix. Fertilize and water well, for a plentiful supply of foliage throughout summer. The tarragon and thymes are perennial plants, which can stay in the window box year after year. Dill is an annual; it will die off in the fall and should be replaced with fresh plants in spring. Parsley is biennial; it will flower and die in its second year, when it should be replaced

Or you could try growing these plants in a trough and stand it next to the barbecue so you have fresh herbs to hand where you need them most.

A	B	C	B	A
D	E	D	E	D

two peas in a pod

You need

6 pea 'Half Pint' **A**

6 *Lathyrus odoratus*
'Cupid' (sweet pea) **B**

This endearing hanging basket combines decorative, scented sweet peas with real garden peas—true cottage-style garden charm. Pick both flowers and peas regularly, for a steady supply of both throughout summer.

Planting & care Plant the hanging basket in late spring, when all risk of frost has passed. Use a fertile, moisture-retentive potting mix, and add some well-rotted compost if possible. Keep the potting mix moist at all times, and fertilize regularly, to keep the flowers and peas coming. Remove the sweet pea flowers as they die, to encourage more blooms. Pick the garden peas as soon as they are large enough—they will be so sweet you won't be able to resist eating them straight from the plant.

Or you could try planting asparagus peas (*Lotus tetragonolobus*) instead. This unusual but highly decorative vegetable has very pretty, red flowers and delicious, winged pods.

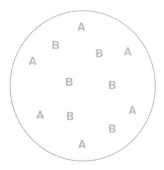

sweet sensation

You need

9 strawberry 'Aromel' **A**

Strawberries growing in a hanging basket are easy to harvest, the precious fruits stay clean and dry, and, perhaps most importantly, the slugs can't reach them. Choose an everbearing variety and you'll be harvesting sweet fruits through summer and the fall.

Planting & care Plant the hanging basket in the fall, with the base of each crown level with the surface of the potting mix. Choose a moisture-retentive potting mix, to which you have added some extra compost and a sprinkling of bonemeal. Water and fertilize regularly in spring and summer, but avoid wetting the plants' leaves. Remove any runners that appear, to preserve the plants' energy. Pick the fruits as they ripen. In the fall, cut off the old foliage and apply a balanced fertilizer.

Or you could try growing a June-fruiting variety rather than an everbearing strawberry, for a larger summer crop. Try 'Hapil' or 'Cambridge Favorite'.

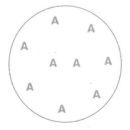

tumbling tomatoes

You need

2 *Petroselinum crispum*
(parsley) **A**

2 *Thunbergia alata*
(black-eyed Susan vine) **B**

2 tomato 'Tumbling Tom
Red' **C**

2 tomato 'Tumbling Tom
Yellow' **D**

A vibrant mixture of red and yellow tomatoes, curly parsley, and black-eyed Susan vine makes a fine display for a hanging basket. These bushy, little tomato plants produce masses of juicy, cherry-sized fruits from summer to the fall.

Planting & care Plant up the basket in late spring, when all risk of frost has passed. Use rich, moisture-retentive potting mix to which you have added some water-retaining crystals. Line the basket with polyethylene, to retain moisture. Fertilize and water regularly as the plants are growing. Water consistently when the fruits appear: erratic watering can cause them to split. Pick the parsley as you need it, and harvest the tomatoes as they ripen. Discard the plants in the fall.

Or you could try growing peppers in the basket instead of tomatoes. Choose compact, bushy varieties, such as sweet pepper 'Minimix', which produces lots of little peppers in shades of red, orange, and green; or chili pepper 'Prairie Fire' which will be covered in mini, red fruits with a hot, fiery flavor.

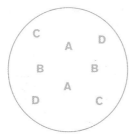

index

acknowledgments

Publisher Jane Birch
Managing editor Clare Churly
Design manager Tokiko Morishima
Designer Ginny Zeal
Picture library assistant Ciaran O'Reilly
Senior production controller Manjit Sihra

photography

Alamy Holmes Garden Photos 46; Keith Mindham 203; Mark Bolton Photography 69;

Andrew Lawson Andrew Lawson 51, 51, 52, 53, 143, 153, 155, 157; Paul Williams 211; Powis Castle 148;

Clive Nichols Clive Nichols 55, 61, 92, 107, 130, 139;

Gap Photos Elke Borkowski 75; FhF Greenmedia 199; Francois De Heel 149; Friedrich Strauss 58, 67, 73, 85, 88, 115, 129, 158, 167; Graham Strong 29, 31, 35, 41, 91, 95, 125, 135, 161, 173, 183, 185, 205, 207, 223; Howard Rice 27; J S Sira 113, 215; Jerry Harpur 189, 217; John Glover 221; Mark Bolton 99; Richard Bloom 187, 201;

GardenPhotoLibrary Derek St. Romaine 219;

Harpur Garden Library Jerry Harpur 133; Marcus Harpur 25, 175, 177, 193;

Marianne Majerus 45;

Octopus Publishing Group Limited 144; Diana Beddoes 137; Freia Turland 8, 10, 13, 14, 16, 18, 18, 21, 140, 212, 225, 227, 229, 231, 233; Mark Bolton 82, 82;

Photolibrary Claire Davies 121; Graham Strong 22, 43, 65; Howard Rice 49, 71; John Glover 165, 179; Lynne Brotchie 181;

Photoshot Michael Warren 87, 103;

The Garden Collection Andrew Lawson 33, 37, 57, 81, 111,119, 171; Derek Harris 77, 79; Liz Eddison 39, 97, 101, 109, 117, 123, 162, 163, 197; Marie O' Hara 127, 190, 195, 209; Nicola Stocken Tomkins 63, 105, 147